MEDITATION
Myths & Reality

MEDITATION
Myths & Reality

Harish Malik

STERLING PUBLISHERS (P) LTD.
Regd. Ofice: A1/256 Safdarjung Enclave, New Delhi-110029.
Cin: U22110DL1964PTC211907
Mobile: +91 82877 98380/+91 120-6251823
e-mail: mail@sterlingpublishers.in
www.sterlingpublishers.in

Meditation: Myths & Reality
© 2021, Rani Malik
ISBN 978 81 950824 8 3

All rights are reserved.
No part of this publication may be reproduced, stored in a retrieval system or transmitted, in any form or by any means, mechanical, photocopying, recording or otherwise, without prior written permission of the original publisher.

Printed and Published in India by

Sterling Publishers Pvt. Ltd.,
Plot No. 13, Ecotech-III, Greater Noida -201306, U. P. India

Foreword

Harish Malik and I were together in the 1952–1954 class of MA English Literature at Delhi University. He was a brilliant student and had stood third in the University in the graduation exam.

His brilliance manifested itself soon enough through the force of his personality and he got a job in Air India. He was very hardworking and his sincere work saw him reach the No. 2 position as Director, Commercial by 1985 or so. He was posted in several countries as Regional Director, and blazed a new trail wherever he went.

He developed an interest in meditation around 1993 and soon his involvement in this field grew immensely. He would meditate frequently – at times for hours. We all know the importance of meditation in restoring equanimity and mental balance.

Harish Malik died in 2003 in an unfortunate accident. He had written a treatise on meditation. Rani, his wife, and Priya, his daughter, handed over the manuscript to me. I was amazed at the insights presented and thought it should be published for posterity.

The treatise presents a fresh viewpoint of the subject. I do hope the experts will enjoy it.

Krishan Mohan

Prologue

Harish was a multi-faceted person. We married in 1963 and remained so until his passing in 2003. I experienced many aspects of his personality during this time, but none so intriguing as his deep dive into meditation in the last ten years of his life.

One day, while he was sitting on his bed and wondering about existence and the meaning of life, he was seized by an energy – it was an answer, it seemed, from the very depths of God Himself. This energy had a profound effect on his life, providing a deep rasa throughout the rest of his days.

He cultivated the energy through hours of daily meditation and, at some point, began to record his experiences. While this book is a record of what perhaps few people have had the privilege to go through, there were many visible changes that took place in him at the same time. One of them that stood out was the fact that his hair, which was all white, began to become more and more black in his later years.

In reading this book we may surmise how this may have happened, and how it was one of the side-effects of what he had begun to undergo on a daily basis.

I am so grateful to Krishan Mohan ji, a very close friend of Harish from their college days, for helping to get this book published. May it provide some glimpse into the ever-present mystical force that holds and animates us, and with whom we can no doubt develop a deeper relationship if we so will, as perhaps hinted by Harish's experiences.

Rani Malik
12 June 2021

Garden Home 20,
Celebrity Homes, Palam Vihar,
Gurgaon 122017, Haryana.

Contents

Foreword	v
Prologue	vi
1. The Force	1
2. The Journey Continues	49
3. The Reality	70
4. The Transformation	90
5. Consciousness	103
Bibliography	108

The Force

I started meditation in late 1993 on my own after having read a number of books by Indian and foreign writers. I started with concentration on breath and its in-and-out movements. I used to meditate once a day for just 10–15 minutes. However, during my daily walks of over an hour, I concentrated on breath most of the time. It was a pleasurable, sensuous exercise.

After a few months, I began to concentrate on the brow. During my walks, however, I concentrated on external objects like tops of trees, early morning sun and in the evenings on distant electric lights, moon etc. This helped in increasing concentration and also kept my mind still.

Later, during my walks I concentrated on various parts of the body one by one, from the head to the feet and up the same way. This device, as I had read somewhere, helped to develop body consciousness besides concentration. At other times, I began silently to recite the mantra 'Om Namay Shivai' to occupy the mind. I took to mantra as I had read that mantras have special powers and regular reciting of mantras with devotion leads to spiritual development. However, I took to mantra only to still the mind and had no faith in the mantra and gave up this stratagem after a very short period.

Progressively, I began to look more and more within. For quite a long time, endless as it seemed, my mind almost continuously dwelt on the past. I was all the time engaged in analysing my weaknesses and failures, what I should not have done or done differently. I hardly ever thought of good times or achievements. In fact, it seemed as if there had been just no positive occurrences in the past, none whatsoever.

I often wondered whether one's mind is more habituated to recall the unpleasant than the pleasant. Or is it that unpleasant experiences leave a deeper mark than pleasant ones? Or is it that looking within is to learn from the past, not to wallow in it? Or putting it differently, is it that one has to learn only from one's mistakes and that successes or achievements have nothing to teach?

It was a period of intense depression and self-doubt; the entire past life seemed to have been an utter waste and the feeling would leave me empty within. Many a time, and quite uncharacteristically, I felt gripped by a strong death-wish. I have been a highly egotistic person and I think that continuous preoccupation with a failed life bruised my inflated ego, leading to bouts of intense depression.

The sense of having lived a futile existence often gave rise to questions: 'What am I?' 'Who am I?' or 'Why am I here?' I had no answers and would end up with the resolve to find the answers.

I spent hours and hours, day after day, in introspection – just thoughts, and only thoughts, mind full of chaos and a lot of remorse and a sense of self-pity – self-pity because I had myself decided to opt to engage myself as much as possible in looking within. I felt confined, a prisoner of my own self. I could neither give up looking within nor was I able to get rid of the past. I was not ready to start living in the now, detached from the past. The ghosts of past and a deep sense of remorse would leave me totally exhausted.

The only relief was meditation. The mind would be still then, often with an overpowering feeling of being liberated from myself. Meditation became a serious occupation. I slept less and would get up at 3 or 4 in the morning and meditate, lying down in shav asan posture. I would, in these sessions, just observe the vibrations, wherever they moved, and not specifically concentrate on the brow.

I often wondered whether I was really so devoted to meditation that I spent more and more time on it or that I did so because it offered me an escape from myself. I also thought that many others, too, might be taking to meditation to cocoon themselves in their own self to escape from the harsh realities of life, unpleasant past and present, and uncertain future. My views changed later after I began to see a change in my sense of values and perception of life.

I started meditation as an agnostic. I believed that there was a power that ran the universe. The universe moved in an orderly, predictable way – the cycle of day and night and seasons, birth, growth and decay, and so on. I believed that there was a neutral force responsible for the whole phenomenon. This force, I was convinced, was devoid of attributes like mercy, compassion, forgiveness, justice, retribution and the like; and that humans credited the natural force with having the same emotions and attributes as they themselves experienced and called it 'God' in order to feel themselves as being in the image of God and in order to feel elevated.

Humans, in contrast with animals and the plant world, I believed, were equipped by the power that I termed as 'Nature' with a mind to manage their lives themselves. It was the individual mind that, I was convinced, accounted for differences amongst people: happy or miserable, rich or poor, good or bad and the like. Everyone was responsible for his or her own destiny, themselves being its author. I also recognised that childhood environment and upbringing definitely played a part, in one's life particularly in fashioning one's mind.

Religion, according to me, was a human invention, at best, to inject a sense of values among people to impart some orderliness in life and, at worst, for the priestly order and religious heads to control and manipulate people for their selfish interests. Spiritualism had, in my thinking, no meaning and served as an exalted philosophy of the same selfish interests as those promoting religion.

Prayer had no place in my way of thinking, nor was there any logic in thanking Nature or any other power for anything good in life because whatever was there, good or bad, was a person's own doing.

As I went along on the course of increased meditation, I often caught myself spontaneously and involuntarily thanking the power I began calling the 'Divine' for having given the opportunity to me to pursue a new path. Repeatedly, I would spontaneously pray for courage, patience and perseverance. For a long time I continued getting a sense of shock at the sudden, irrational development. It took me quite a while to accept the fact that I had, in spite of myself, changed. My inner self had recognised what my outer self would not, that there was a force that dictated my path and that the inner self was grateful for the change.

Around 1997–98, I started taking yoga lessons from a swami. He asked me to change the meditation technique. He advised me to concentrate on five chakras: brow, throat, heart, abdomen and the lower abdomen, one by one, starting from up to down and then from down to up.

In October 1999, I began to experience a strange and highly disturbing phenomenon. I felt strong vibrations moving constantly within the body. I named it 'The Force'. I would become conscious of its movements when I was physically still like while reading, watching TV, even driving a car or listening to others talk. The Force did not affect my driving because it did not affect physical action.

However, I could not read beyond a few minutes. I had to get up, walk around or engage myself in some kind of physical activity and only then could I resume reading. I had to make a concentrated effort to pay attention to conversations. I could talk easily myself, but had to make an effort to listen to others. The more I would become conscious of the Force, the more forceful and intense would be its movements.

I felt concerned at this phenomenon and talked about it to a friend who had been meditating for over 15 years. He suggested that I visit *Sri Balayogi Ashram* at Dehradun. I visited the ashram twice, in late 1999 and early 2000, and held prolonged discussions with Gen. Hanut Singh and Swami Shivrudra (popularly called Shinooji). The visits were beneficial. I felt reassured that I must continue to pursue the path that I had chosen. I also received some practical suggestions and was advised to meditate on the centre of my brow instead of concentrating on the five chakras. However, I did not get any explanation as to why the Force had suddenly awakened and why I had lost the capacity to concentrate on external things.

In August 2000, I attended my first Vipassana course, in Kathmandu. Its initial technique requires that one should be conscious of one's breath. I could not do it constantly because when I sat still, I would become conscious of the movements of the Force. It was just not possible for me to ignore the Force.

A later Vipassana technique requires that one should move one's attention over the whole body, part by part, except the genitals, and halt to concentrate on areas where there is a resistance till the resistance subsides or gets reduced. The idea is to experience smooth flow of one's attention. I found that, at times, I could follow this technique. More often, however, I could not do so as the Force would be active and carry out its own programme of movements.

One evening, towards the end of the Kathmandu course, I decided to let the Force have a free play. I found that it moved from one part of the body to another, systematically clearing up denseness and resistance, part by part, with more effective results than deliberate movement of attention over the body.

I came back from Kathmandu in mid-August. I continued to pursue this technique and gave up the technique of concentration on the brow. I thought that an essential prerequisite for real or significant spiritual advancement was the conscious removal of denseness from the entire physical system.

I am not a follower of Vipassana for many reasons. However, I found Vipassana worthwhile for two reasons. One, for ten long days, from 4.30 a.m. to 10 p.m. each day, all one is engaged in is meditation. One is not allowed to engage in any other activity such as reading, writing, listening to radio, etc. Two, one has to maintain complete silence throughout – no communication with other course-mates, not even eye contact because that too is communication, and no phone calls. One can only talk to the course teacher to provide feedback on progress or any problems being faced.

I decided to attend another Vipassana course in October 2000 in Gurgaon. During this course, the Force became more active. I found that I was not able to sleep, particularly when I lay flat on my back, due to frequent and rather aggressive movements of the Force. I had to lie down sideways, mostly on my left shoulder, to get some sleep. My total sleep became very little, often as little as 2–3 hours a day.

Inability to sleep caused considerable distress. Apart from a sense of lethargy and fatigue during the day, I was mentally disturbed.

The Force

In the Vipassana course, every evening there is an audio-visual talk by S.N. Goenka, the chief of Vippasana and its founder in India. In one of the talks, he briefly mentioned about the problem of sleeplessness. He said that meditation could cause sleeplessness but it should not cause mental distress. The objective of sleep, as we experience it daily, is, he said, to rest physically and mentally. When one lies down for 5-6 hours continuously, the body gets rested and if one concentrates on vibrations, the mind takes rest, as the mind is then inactive. Though I felt reassured that mine was not a unique development or that sleeplessness was not a health hazard, I was still concerned as to why the particular development had taken place in me.

I discussed the matter with the Vippasana course teacher. He said that I could not let myself be ruled by the Force. There were many instances of people losing control of themselves, mentally or physically, due to meditation. He quoted the case of his own brother who became a victim of serious digestive problems resulting in continuous illness and severe ill-health. There was another case of a person in his village who became mentally affected and deranged.

The teacher, in all sincerity, felt that it was essential that I stay in control of my own self. He felt that I should try to use my Vipassana will and channelise the activity of the Force. If that was not possible then, he felt, I should give up meditation for a couple of months and resume when I could meditate in my own way and do whatever else I wanted to without hindrance.,

I decided to ignore the advice. Firstly, I had tasted some of the benefits of meditation. Secondly since 1993, when I began meditation, I had, over time, come to believe that it was best for me to flow with life as it unfolded rather than direct it myself. I had, after all, made a mess of my life by trusting my own judgment and being obsessed with doing things my own way. Going over the past I realised that all the major, significant events in my life happened accidentally and my own planning and initiatives had proved of no worth, I had come to the decision that I would no longer initiate things; I would just respond to life's initiatives. I felt that if providence willed that I should suffer physically or become mentally unfit or deranged, then so be it and I would let the Divine will prevail.

I was also reminded of what Gen. Hanut Singh in Dehradun said when I mentioned that the awakening of kundalini could, I believed, cause serious health problems as in the case of Pandit Gopi Krishna. Gen. Hanut Singh tersely remarked – how could the pursuit of Divine result in any form of distress?

I felt that I must have at some stage followed wrong meditation techniques and I should, therefore, seek advice from someone who could put me on the right course.

I talked to Chitvan and Pravir about the problem and of the advice that I was given by the Vipassana teacher. I sought their assistance in finding someone experienced meditation in Puducherry and they introduced me to Sraddhalu.

Sraddhalu asked me to change my technique. At that time, I used to meditate on the centre of my brow. He suggested that I concentrate on the heart-centre. This method, he said, helped in awakening and developing the psyche. In regard to sleeplessness, Sraddhalu suggested that before going to sleep, I should pray to the Force to let me sleep. I started doing that every night and was amazed to find that the prayer worked. Though I was still not able to sleep when I lay flat, I started sleeping for much longer time.

I felt as if I was being punished for some specific wrong or the past way of life. I felt possessed by the Force. I had the option to give up meditation temporarily or forever,

The Force

as the Vipassana teacher had suggested, or to live with the situation. I felt had no other option but to continue with meditation.

What was this Force? How and why did it suddenly become active? What was its role? And why in me? Would it ever go away? These and other similar questions kept on coming to my mind. The issues got clarified on their own as I continued to look within.

In fact, I realised later that it was the Force that compelled me to keep on looking within by its incessant activity and, therefore, for a change in my sense of values and way of life, imparting a new meaning and purpose to life.

How does regular, continued 'looking within' bring about a change in sense of values and the way of life? What happens inside? I would constantly ask myself. At one stage I thought that two factors were responsible for the phenomenon.

One was that constant looking within gradually sharpens introspectiveness. By microscopically looking at one's past happenings at each step – thoughts, emotions, actions, reactions – in the present context, one begins to analyse objectively all personal situations and identify the wrongs and the rights. Gradually, one begins to see a pattern in one's behaviour and the set of standard and pet responses to particular types of situations. This automatically leads to handling similar situations differently, when they arise again.

The second factor, I thought, was the clearing up or removal of denseness in the body. Whether one follows the Vipassana way of concentrating on different parts of the body in rotation, that I began to feel later created its own problems if followed constantly, or on the brow or heart-centre, concentration activates the Force that clears up deposits of denseness in the body.

None of the books, more than a dozen, that I have read on meditation, refer to denseness in the body. The only explanation I came across was in the Vipassana course. Vipassana says that denseness is produced by unwholesome feelings, reactions or responses such as greed, craving, jealousy, anger and the like. Like all teachers of meditation who as a matter of rule are wont to just to proffer advice as to what or what not to do without explaining the reasons, the Vipassana, too, only says that unwholesome emotions and thoughts produce denseness. Vipassana does not say what is the effect of these emotions and thoughts on the body that results in the production of denseness nor does it clarify what denseness is made of and how and why it disintegrates when one meditates and other related questions. I think that the unwholesome thoughts and emotions produce certain chemicals in the body that are responsible for the denseness.

I found that concentration with a still mind on the chosen spot or even roving attention to the movements of the Force removes denseness, part-by-part and layer-by-layer. As denseness goes away, one feels lighter not only physically but also emotionally and mentally, often experiencing a sense of joy, an inner joy totally unconnected with external situation. In the initial stages, habituated to feelings of happiness only in pleasant situations, I would look for external factors that could have been the source of joy. I would be amazed to realise that there was nothing in the outside world for me to feel happy about. In the initial stages, the sense of joy comes and goes. Ultimately, I believe, it is there all the time.

Joy is an unusual and special experience, qualitatively vastly different from the sense of happiness that one normally feels. It is a mellow feeling that fills up the whole being and it comes suddenly and without a rational cause and disappears as suddenly as it comes.

The Force

As denseness goes away, the physical system gets cleaned up and purified: ears, nose, eyes, throat, bowels, etc. I experienced a variety of developments during the purification like eruption of boils in different parts of the body, frequent sore throat, running nose, frequent prolonged sneezing fits, watering of eyes, frequent urination, changes in bowel movements and structure of stools, swelling of limbs and so on.

Most importantly, one develops a different perception of life, a change in the sense of values, growing detachment towards material things and a strong pull for a simpler way of life.

The sense of joy too, I think, is the outcome of the triangular activity – removal of denseness and physical cleansing and, consequently, a feeling of physical, emotional and mental lightness combined with a sense of liberation through shedding of old ways, perceptions and values.

At one stage, I thought that denseness was like vapour or fog or mist. The idea that it was a fog or mist appeared quite attractive. The feeling of lightness – physical, emotional and mental – is as if a heavy weight or cloud has been lifted from the whole being. Denseness, in my case, was thin like fog or vapour, easy to lift, but only in the initial stages. As the Force dug deeper and deeper, denseness turned out to be quite a different entity, thick and hard, like a rock at many a place, difficult to be pierced, extracted and removed.

In fact, denseness had spread all over the body by an intricate web of cris-cross, interlinked strands running across the entire body, right from head down to the through the soles and to the upper part of the feet and similarly through the palms and back of hands to all the five fingers of both the hands. There were cob-like webs of thin strands between the heels and tips of all the toes, more prominently the big and little toes. There were similar webs of strands in the hands. These webs were on both the upper and lower sides of feet and hands. What these webs actually were became clear later.

There were layers and layers of denseness all over the body, except eyelids that had just a single thin film of denseness found in the initial stages. Initially I thought that there were layers only in the front part of the body. However, in the later stages, I found numerous layers extending from the back of head to the hips. The layers on the back were thick sheets or walls, many more in number and much tougher than the layers in front.

Unlike the front, it appeared that the back was also riddled with a few strands of denseness. I found later that there were no strands on the back. As layer after layer of denseness got removed from the front, the main strands, too, moved down and the downward pressure of vibrations gave the impression of independent strands in the back. In the final stages, however, the strands performed a double role, clearing denseness both from the front and the back wherever there was a requirement.

In addition, there were rings of denseness all over the body, from the lower part of the chest down to the pelvic nerve, a ring across each ankle and others above the ankles, knees, upper thighs, neck and around each shoulder, arm joints, elbows and wrists. In course of time many additional rings came to light, both below the pelvic nerve and above the neck.

The whole body had a thick lining of denseness forming a border all around the body. The border started from a ring around the head, above the ears, down each shoulder to the feet, covering inner and outer sides of the arms, thighs and legs and inner thighs, joined together with a band below the lower end of the spinal cord. The border was hard, particularly around the feet.

The Force

There were many junctions, mostly at both ends of main nerves – spots where three or four or more strands met. Many of the junctions were deep, entangled knots. The knotted junctions were extra hard and difficult to dismantle, involving prolonged laborious effort. The extreme cases were junctions at each outer ankle, outer knee, outer wrist and the right-side ends of hips and the pelvic nerve. The most difficult ones were the junctions at the front and back lower part of both the shoulders, hips and the lower edges of the neck. In the final stages, I identified as many as 16 junctions on each side of the body after a large number observed earlier had disintegrated.

There were two types of strands – main strands and shoots or subsidiary strands. The network of strands was a large and extensive, reaching each and every nook and corner of the body. All the main strands were interconnected with one another.

At one stage, a little before the removal of all denseness, I identified seven main strands with umpteen number of shoots that passed through a large number of junctions. Main strands kept on sliding lower and lower, layer by layer, but most of the shoots disintegrated along with the removal of the connected layer. All the seven strands merged along the way with one or more than one main strand. Thus, all seven main strands were a part of one integrated network that I termed as the 'Strands System' that reached through other connected strands to almost the whole of the body. I called the individual main strands along with their off shoots as 'sections'. All the sections appeared in the beginning to be loops on their own or through combination with others. Actually, except sections three and seven, others were not loops and directly terminated in and originated from the top of the head. In the final stages, I could identify ten strands, five on each side, that terminated in the crown.

The sections were present thus:

Section One: Two strands from top of the head, down each shoulder to the inner hips and pelvis and down to the heels. Besides many subsidiary strands on the way, there were four very tough junctions on each side – at the outer hip-bone and pelvis, outer side of knee and outer ankle. In addition, each heel was connected with top of the head via each shoulder by two strands – one connected with the left and the other with the right shoulder. These two, as I found later, also terminated at top of the head. Two more strands from top of the head moved down via each end of the collar-bone and were tied up in junctions beneath knee caps, on their way to the feet.

Section Two: Two strands from top of the head to the shoulders, each across to the other side hip-bone where it split into two strands, one down to the right and the other to the left knee and heel. This section joined Section One at the hip-bone junction on each side. There was a tough knot near the heart-centre where the two crossing strands from shoulders met the Section Six main strand. This section was one of the toughest section.

Section Three: Two loops on each side from top of the head down via the collar-bone to beneath pelvis bone ring and up to head lop again via the back. The front strands of the loops extended down to each heel and thus joined Section One there. It also passed though the loop of the Section Four.

Section Four: Two strands from head-top to around the prostrate and the area surrounding the testes. The top parts of strands were also tied to Section One at the two junctions on each side of hip-bone and thus became part of Section One. Two strands from the lower side ends of the Section joined up with rings around each thigh.

Section Five: A ring around the neck. The main strands from all the above four Sections passed through the nerve where the collar-bone is and some also via the back of neck. Thus, this section was also connected to the top of the head.

Section Six: It appeared as a loop over the back and front of the spinal cord. This loop extended beyond the length of spinal cord at both the upper and the lower ends – the upper part to the crown of the head and the lower part well beyond the end of the spinal cord. This strand, in fact, was not a loop. Because of its strategic location in the middle of the body and as it extended beyond the spinal cord at both the ends, this strand played a very vital role in the clearance of denseness.

Two nerves became noticeable near the end of all denseness. These nerves ran parallel to the spinal cord on each side and were exactly of the same length as the spinal cord.

Section Seven: This consisted of two loops each at shoulder-arm joint. There were two junctions – one each in the front and the back, and both were extremely tough. There were of a number of nerves observed in various Sections. The two cross-way nerves in Section One joined the junction in the front and travelled further to the backside junction then onto the crown. Two nerves referred to in Section One that extended to the inner hips and then to the feet were also a part of the front junction. Two or three nerves on the back were a part of the back junctions.

All the strands, main and subsidiary, were unbreakable. Some of them become thinner in course of time. All of them including the main strands were deflected or dilate under pressure of heavy denseness or intense vibrations. Some of the strands, mostly the left side strands, occasionally shifted towards the right and passed through the mouth, over the tongue, or touched the palate on their way to the forehead or the neck. I found them sharp like a knife.

The strands had some very distinctive features. Some were very thin but others appeared thick like ropes. Irrespective of the thickness, all were tough and unbreakable and had sharp, cutting edges. As all denseness disappeared, many strands that I called subsidiary also disappeared. Many remained till the end of all the denseness. All strands in the Strands System originated from the head or the brain.

The strands, their characteristics and network, were an intriguing phenomenon and I was very curious to find out what they were made of, what caused them to cover the whole body so extensively, how was it that some disappeared early and others stayed till the last vestige of denseness, etc. After some investigation, including reading of medical books and discussions with neurologists, I concluded that the strands were nerves that constitute the sensory and communication network of the physical system. Most of them originate in the brain. According to medical science, nerves do not shift position. However, I am sure that they shift position, and an explanation that they do shift, as I actually experienced, is given later in this book.

It is not possible for me to be absolutely sure about the accuracy of all the details in the Strands System or of individual sections for a number of reasons. The strands appeared to keep on shifting their positions, making it difficult to be sure about their precise location. Moreover, a number of them disappeared with progressive removal of denseness. An important point is that meditation is concentration on the chosen spot. Though one may be conscious of happenings in the other parts of the body yet, as the main attention is riveted on one spot, one cannot be too sure about the number or location of individual strands.

However, three factors helped me in getting a fairly good idea of the strands network. The first factor was that I spent a good amount of time every day on, what

The Force

I call, 'free' or preferably 'roving' meditation in addition to, for want of better description, 'one-spot' meditation Roving meditation viz. letting the Force move wherever it wanted to, drew a sort of a daily map of the entire inside, in addition to the identification of the remaining difficult areas. In other words, it took stock of daily progress. At times, it also gave a quick, short glimpse of developments which would take place in the future.

The second factor was daily the yoga asanas. I have been doing yoga for years with occasional gaps of varying duration. In one of the early meetings, Sraddhalu suggested that I should do yoga every day. I had suspended doing yoga at that time and did not pay attention to Sraddhalu's advice. In a subsequent meeting after about three months, Sraddhalu asked me whether I had re-started yoga. As Sraddhalu seemed insistent, I started doing yoga again.

I found that yoga was a great help. In fact, Sraddhalu had said that yoga was a part and parcel of meditation, 'an offering of the body to the Divine'.

Yoga helped in expediting the process of clearing denseness. Unlike the past when I performed asanas rapidly one after another, more as physical exercise, I began to do them slowly, deliberately spending time at remaining stationary in the final position of each asana. I could feel the nerves that were still immersed in denseness in each and every asana. In the final of postures of asanas, the nerves would pulsate, displacing the surrounding denseness. For me, yoga was an extension of meditation in that I continuously looked within to watch the performance of the nerves and the results achieved. By the time I would finish a yoga session, I would get an up-to-date position – a daily stock position, of the areas yet to be cleared.

The third factor was the daily water therapy. I drank 2–3 litres of water every morning on an empty stomach, usually after a couple of meditation sessions. Besides cleaning the system, the water would travel to all the areas that had been cleared of denseness during the morning meditation and show up the nerves and the remaining dense parts. The water also helped in washing away the dislodged impurities in the form of mucus through the nose, sneezing fits and watering of the eyes and the nose. Obviously, the eyes and the nose dislodged impurities from the head and the impurities from the lower parts of the body passed through urine and stool. In fact, there were frequent changes in the structure of my stool in conformity with the type of denseness that was being cleared. For example, it would be hard and thick or sticky depending on whether hard and thick or sticky denseness got cleared

A few features relating to heavy denseness need to be recorded. I noticed that the soles of my feet had gauze or cobweb-like spread of strands. I later discovered that there was a direct link between these cobwebs and similar but much wider cobwebs on both the sides of the forehead. and mid and lower temples. The forehead cobwebs were further connected with similar cobwebs in the right and left sides groin and these were further connected with two spreads covering all the sides of the shoulders. Of course, all the cobwebs or nets on the right side were much thicker. However, not one of the four spreads got cleared in spite of many attempts. Later, I realised that the four cobwebs were actually not cobwebs; they were spreads of thin nerves that came into prominence due to heavy denseness in the areas.

I came across two more astonishing developments. One was that two masses of thin nerves in the front, from the head down to the area below the end of spinal cord and across to the thighs, were joined together on both the left and the right side. Moreover, the two nerve masses were hooked to each other in between at numerous places. The four cobwebs noted earlier were a part of one of the thin nerves mass. The joining up of the two nerve masses compressed the entire front part of the body; most of the junctions became tighter, particularly at the hips, pelvis bone and front and back shoulder junctions, so firmly as to make their removal another extremely tedious and difficult operation. Later, I got the impression that there was an additional nerves mass at the back.

The second feature was a thick coat of denseness that fully covered the ears, the left one more thickly than the right ear. Subsequently, I found that this shroud-like cover stretched all the way from the head down to the feet, mostly on the back of the body. However, the cover was thinner on the rest of the body than on the ears. This denseness was qualitatively different. It was elastic and tough like rubber. It would loosen under the impact of vibrations but it disintegrated extremely slowly, only after repeated attempts. Its thickness varied from part to part, extremely thick in the head, as well as all round the neck and the front and the back of the upper chest area, besides the ears.

This peculiar phenomenon, along with the irksome and mildly painful passage of nerves though the mouth and throat was so odd that I often doubted whether these and other odd happenings were actually there or whether they were a product of my overheated imagination. Apprehensive that if the nerves were actually there in the middle of the mouth and throat, I would not be able to eat or breathe properly, I would often stop meditation to check and would be relieved to find that the mouth and throat functioned normally. That there were two mouths, throats or other sensitive parts, ones during meditation that felt the nerves passing through them and the other during normal activity without the nerves seemed like a magician's trick and needed a rational explanation. The explanation emerged later.

At one stage I came to believe that my right side had much more of denseness, much thicker and harder, than the left side. The remarkable aspect of this feature was that the area around the heart had no denseness though the left shoulder and the upper areas in the front and back had plenty of solidified rubber-like thickness. As the process of removal of denseness often puts considerable pressure on the spot involved, it is obvious that the heart region was an out-of-bounds area for denseness, so as not to strain the heart.

I raised the matter of greater denseness on the right side with the Vipassana teacher and with Sraddhalu. However, neither of them could provide a clarification. In fact, Sraddhalu said that normally there should be equal amount of denseness on either side. In the later stages of my tumultuous journey, I found that whilst the of shoots of the main strands on the right side ran sideways further right or up or down, the shoots of strands on the left cut across to the right side, thus making the denseness on the right side appear thicker, tougher and more difficult to negotiate. With more experience, I realised that it was not that the of shoots from the left came across to the right side; it was that masses of dislodged denseness from the left moved over to the right side. A fuller explanation of apparently less denseness on the left side emerged later as I progressed further that clarified that I was under an erroneous impression that the left side had less amount of denseness.

***

I became conscious of denseness around six years after I started meditation. For most of these six years, the vibrations were mostly gentle and rarely forceful till the Force became prominent. When the Force became noticeably active and dominant, gentle vibrations almost disappeared, replaced by forceful and often aggressive ones, and not only during meditation but during all the conscious time. However, I was still not conscious of any denseness in the body.

The Force

The first time I became aware of denseness was when I attended the first Vipassana course in August 2000. The Vipassana technique is that one should concentrate on the body, part by part. One would experience some resistance in the movement of concentration in certain spots due to the presence of denseness. One should halt at such spots till the resistance disappears and then move on. Would it be that had I not attended the Vipassana course I would have never become conscious of denseness? This is unlikely, given the heavy, all pervasive denseness in my body and my consequent numerous experiences. I believe that denseness exists in every human body and that denseness must be cleared to reach anywhere near the goal to achieve self-awareness. After all, the Vipassana technique is for everyone and would not be so unless there is denseness in the human body. Yet, why is it that not one of the dozen and more of the authors I have read on meditation talks of denseness? Is it that everyone need not ever become conscious of denseness and yet reach somewhere? The answer would obviously depend on the level of denseness in the individual physical system.

Denseness, I found, was of many types depending on the age and location of deposits. It was soft and thin like vapour as in the uppermost layers that obviously were freshly produced. It was like a thick fog or mist that at times is so solid that one cannot see beyond a yard or two. Yet when thick fog disappears, it leaves nothing behind except traces of water and some dust particles. Denseness too disappeared the same way leaving no trace, as such, of having been there. Thick denseness was in the lower layers. Lower the layer, thicker, harder and more solidified was the denseness. Denseness at some places was like a stone and, at times, left behind bits of pieces stuck in the body for days. I had two such experiences. In some areas, denseness was sticky and glued to the skin or bones. It was also both sticky and viscous like rubber in other places like – the denseness covering both the ears and other parts of the body noted earlier and more so on the left side. Denseness underneath the sexual organs and rectum was particularly sticky and viscous.

The denseness that covered the gauze-like cobwebs and was stuck to the thin nerves-masses at the back and in the front and made the two masses join together, was sticky like glue and thick and seemed to be ribbed in some places as if bearing the imprint of thin nerves that it covered.

It is said that the universe is made up of five elements: earth, water, fire, air and ether. I think that denseness, too, is made up of the same five elements with a variable measure of a mix of different elements depending on the type of denseness. The upper soft layers have perhaps more or all of water and air and the lower, thick layers have more of earth and less of other elements. Ether is like light that is believed to spread awareness in the body. Would, then, ether be a constituent of denseness – an unwholesome substance? Maybe. Maybe the energy of the Force ignited the fire that, along with the other four elements, was an ingredient of denseness. All other elements got burnt out making the body actually warm, and at times so hot as if the body was on fire and, I think, that only ether remained to carry on the process of self-awareness. This assumption made considerable sense to me.

Medical science says that certain emotions like anger, hatred and excessive desire produce certain chemicals in the body that, when, produced regularly and in large measure, lead to hypertension in certain types of persons. These emotions are the same as those which Vipassana classifies as unwholesome and that, according to Vipassana, produce denseness. It is therefore reasonable to assume that the chemicals that are the cause of hypertension may also be a factor in the production of denseness. These chemicals may either be the sixth ingredient in denseness or may be just a pollutant in one or more of the five elements.

The Force

Another contributory factor that, as Sraddhalu advised me, produced denseness was rich, fatty and spicy food and food or drinks that produce acidity in the body.

Clearance of denseness was a simple, easy matter when it was soft, as in the uppermost layers. It was not so in respect of the lower layers. In my case, the lower layers had umpteen strands, rings, junctions and knots. The rings around the feet, knees, thighs, wrists and shoulders, along with the junctions were like straps around the body and the junctions were like nuts and bolts. I was literally bound hands and feet. The whole body had sheets and sheets of thick denseness at the back as if to nail me down to a cross. My past lifestyle, it seemed, was determined to hold the inner self as a hapless captive and leave no scope for it to escape.

Strands were the nerves that were coated with denseness and were deflected due to heavy, all round denseness, particularly the denseness underneath the nerves that pushed them off-course. All the nerves in the Strand System and some others that became noticeable later were badly deflected or twisted, some as much as by an inch. They were held in the widely off-course paths by numerous junctions, rings and by being hooked to other off-course nerves. As layers after layers lifted, the process of removal of denseness became harder and harder because the removal of each layer pushed the nerves lower and lower, reducing the space for movement of pulsating vibrations. Thus, each progressive step towards the goal of freedom from denseness became more and more strenuous, often making me actually perspire.

Hard, strenuous work was not limited to just the one-spot meditation. The Force worked all the time either to finish off the unfinished clearing of a layer or to prepare ground for work at the next one-spot meditation session. Even in sleep I was often conscious of the Force at work. Many a time, I would wake up with a sense of heaviness in the chest, full of denseness and felt compelled to get up and meditate to clear up the congestion. Every session, whether one-spot or roving meditation, would leave me fatigued. Before the final stages, I used to meditate for about an hour at a time. In the final stages, I could not sit through for more than half-an-hour and at times just 15 minutes or so at a time. My sleep time again got reduced. I could not read with full concentration either. It was a very difficult, trying period and I would frequently beseech the Force to have mercy and rid me of the ongoing ordeal.

***

Based on certain positive developments, I thought in August 2001 that the final stage of the removal of all denseness would not last for more than a week or two. However, the end to the final stage kept on receding further and further. During this period, whenever there was heavy clearance of denseness in certain crucial parts of the body, particularly the brain, I felt that I would now cruise along to the end. A couple of times, I set up a plan to leave station to attend to outstanding commitments that required concentrated attention. I had to cancel the plans at the last minute as I continued to remain in the midst of the turmoil. Every time a few layers would get cleared, I confronted fresh roadblocks, the most difficult task being the straightening out of the twisted nerves. The Force, it seemed, was bent upon taking its pound of flesh for the past style of life.

It was, however, remarkable that each time I felt down and out, there was immediate, positive breakthrough, a gleam of light to dispel the gloom and frustration. There were far too many such instances to be dismissed as coincidences. I believe that it was the Force itself that would light up the path whenever there was gloom. Gradually, I developed a strong faith that no matter how long the path was and no matter how many obstacles came on the way, the Force would continue to guide me through to the end.

***

The Force

Clearance of denseness had other lessons. Much against my normal nature, I began to recognise the value of patience. I learnt to accept the fact that if the preliminary stage itself was so difficult, so tiresome and frustrating, full of so many trials and tribulations and ups-and-downs and so very long that it took nearly two years, the future course would demand much greater patience, perseverance and mental equilibrium. At a more basic level, I became increasingly more conscious of my body and its value as an instrument of self-awareness and spiritual growth.

I came to believe that it was the destiny of humans to develop spiritually in the same manner as to develop physically, emotionally and mentally. After all, there was nothing special or unique about me. On the contrary, given my past performance, lifestyle, attitude and behaviour, I was just not the type that could ever be imagined to turn around to pursue the spiritual path. Had human selectors been the evaluators, I would have been straightaway rated a totally unsuitable candidate for spiritual development and rejected out of hand. Yet the Force awakened and carried me on and on, on forceful and often very rough currents, to dig deeper and deeper within myself. Obviously, the urge to look within was embedded within. It was either the past karma or my heritage or the self, saturated with excessive externalism, or a combination of two or all the three factors, that shook the Force out of its slumber to take charge and push me on to a new path.

***

The removal of denseness was a fascinating process: sequential, coordinated operation, part-by-part, layer-by-layer, maintaining a balance between the right and the left sides, and the upper and lower areas. It was first the lower parts and then the upper ones and parts on the right first and then the left side that got cleared. However, the situation got reversed in the last stages when it was the left side and the upper parts that got cleared first and the right side and the lower parts later. In fact, the entire sequential coordinated process went to pieces for a time in the final stages during disentanglement of bonded, thin nerve masses in the front and in the back. Many parts at that time got cleared bit-by-bit as isolated units.

The breathing process, taking the breath in and out, heaves the body up and down. During meditation, the breathing slows down with gentle heaving. Both during the one-spot and roving meditation, the heaving operation sent out vibrations sideways and up and down. The upward vibrations moved the upper denseness further up and some of the displaced denseness, that in the breathing process initially moved down, subsequently got pulled or pushed up to fill the vacated space. It was a cyclical operation. Waves of denseness in the front moved up and pushed the head back; the head exerted pressure on the back, temporarily pushing denseness downward, which on reaching lower, in turn, pushed the lower front part of the body up, sending waves of denseness upward again. Most of the denseness, I would say almost all, disintegrated only when it reached the head.

The clearance of rings and junctions was a particularly interesting phenomenon. With each layer, a thin layer of denseness came off as a lesser, attenuated ring. Similarly, a small lump of denseness would become disentangled from the block of denseness covering a junction. Whilst the main rings and junctions stayed intact, the lesser rings and junctions got pulled or sucked up. The suction process was a difficult, effortful and often prolonged exercise and many a time I was not able to pull the lesser rings and junctions to the head, the disintegration zone, in a single session. Whenever this happened, the lesser rings and junctions would slip back to their earlier position, entailing another tedious and tiresome session to disintegrate them.

The Force

In Nature's law, every occurrence is one complete whole. There is no division of up and down, positive and negative and even good or bad. It is the human mind that sees things in parts and divisions. In fact, everything that seems positive or good also has a negative or bad side and vice versa. Similarly, though the disintegration of rings and junctions, main or lesser ones, appeared a tiresome ordeal, it was the rings and junctions that turned out to be the instrument of removal of solidified blocks of denseness in the upper regions by forcefully pushing them upward during their own upward climb. But for the rings and junctions, it would have been very difficult if not impossible to clear the solidified blocks in the upper regions.

The most dramatic part was removal of denseness from the areas below the lower end of the spinal cord. These parts had large deposits of sticky, viscous denseness. In the initial stages, whenever denseness in those parts was under clearance, they would discharge, so it felt, large doses of air that would percolate to the feet and up to the middle body. It felt as if these areas were being aired and cleaned up. Then waves of thick, sticky denseness would spread over these areas, moving slowly to the chest, face and head. The upward movement was remarkably different from the movement of denseness from other parts of the body. It was a step-by-step climb, a step, halt and then another step, in small, short spurts. This denseness would move in forceful waves that would press the body down, particularly the chest and the upper areas. Invariably, a strong shaft of denseness would shoot up to the skull with such pressure that it felt that the shaft would pierce through the skull to go higher and higher out of the body. Unlike other denseness, the columns or shafts of denseness would not wither away after a meditation session; they would stay in position for a considerable time.

In the later stages, the shafts of denseness expanded their role as softeners of particularly hard areas that firmly resisted clearance during one-spot meditation. It is remarkable that the shafts would restrict their work only to soften the denseness in and around the head.

A significant feature of my meditation was that breath always became slow, subdued and gentle. Another remarkable feature was the profuse quantity of saliva in the mouth. This saliva was qualitatively quite different from the normal saliva. It was mildly cool, highly refined and very soothing, and the soothing effect would spread to the head, the entire face and the ears and eyes. However, in the final stages when I came across extremely sticky, solid denseness, I experienced a mildly offensive taste in the mouth, bad odour and often a sickly feeling. Obviously, the deep-down denseness, stored perhaps for years and years, must have become putrid.

Every practitioner of meditation coughs during meditation, some more than others. It is said that a cough is a sign of the weakening resistance of the outer self to give way to the inner self. This is a reasonable but only a symbolic interpretation, typical of Indian spiritual philosophers and gurus who are loath to provide rational explanations. However, the biological fact, as per my experience, was that the cough was due to the shifting of deflected nerves that pass through the throat and/or the bordering areas and in the process put pressure on the throat. I experienced maximum cough on the right side, less on the left and minimum in the middle of the throat. It would seem that there were more deflected nerves on the right side than on the left side or in the middle.

***

Till I switched to concentration on the heart-centre, I was inclined to ignore the lower half of the body for clearance of denseness. Whenever the Force moved downward, I would bring it up. I had the notion that as the nerves emanated from the head it were the upper parts, particularly the head, that were all important and needed greater attention. Little did I realise that the lower half had an equal amount of denseness and that the natural sequence was that denseness from below must move up and put pressure on the denseness in the upper parts to move up to the head to disintegrate there. In fact, it was at the end or final stages that I discovered that the lower parts, the area below the abdomen to the base of the spinal cord and below, had more or less the same type of tough, solidified denseness as the area above the neck.

I found that the Force worked all the time, 24 hours a day. I used to remain gently conscious of its presence during most of the waking time and it would become more and more intensely active when I paid attention to it. The evidence that the Force worked at night too came forward in many ways. In the initial stages, I often felt a gentle tiredness in my feet on waking up in the morning. I did not pay much attention to this phenomenon and only wondered at the strange happening. Later, I began to feel a little heaviness, particularly in the chest area, during the night or on waking up that was not there when I would go to sleep. The heaviness was not of the same kind as one has due to heavy food. This was the heaviness of denseness. Whenever I felt heaviness during the middle of the night, I would wake up and feel compelled to meditate to clear up the denseness. In the final stages, this phenomenon became almost a regular occurrence.

***

It took me a long time to do away with denseness. It was hard work all the way. The spiritually arrived people classify the removal of denseness as a preliminary stage and that is, perhaps, why one does not find it mentioned in any book on meditation. I had excessively high denseness due to a dominantly materialistic and high-profile commercial career. I guess others who seriously set out to pursue the path of inner development lead simple, orderly life. Even if some with a past like mine embarked on a meditation course and experiences problems similar to mine, they would perhaps not pursue the path for long and would give up meditation as I was often advised to do.

There are other reasons for the excessive time to cover the preliminary stage. I changed meditation technique too often. I should have just pursued one technique. Even after I settled down to concentration on the heart-centre. I would, as a reflex action, revert to some of the habits acquired during the earlier meditation techniques. I would let my attention wander to the spot that was under clearness and put pressure on vibrations to clear that spot quickly instead of continued concentration just on the heart-centre. At times, I used my own assessment as to where the vibrations should move and concentrate on that area, my preference being the upper parts to the lower ones.

I realised later, in fact much later, that the best results are achieved through concentration only on the chosen spot. It becomes a vantage point with an overview of the entire field with vibrations moving on their own sideways and up or down sequentially wherever there is a need to tackle denseness. The concentration on one-spot is like an army general conducting a war who has an overview of the entire field through the one-spot and knows when and where action is needed. In contrast when, concentration wanders from scene to scene, it is like fighting individual battles instead of a war, without a sense of priorities and against the natural sequential order.

I was also prone to exert myself to put greater pressure on the spot where an obstruction like a junction or a knot was being tackled. Exertion, I realised much later, is counter-productive. The best results are achieved with gentle, effortless concentration. The Force just wants total concentration – it takes care of the results.

Ancient Indian literature on yoga and meditation recommends body-cleaning and identifies mouth, nose, eyes, throat, stomach and intestines as major parts that should be cleaned through various methods that in modern days appear to be crude and distasteful. A clean body would substantially reduce the level of denseness and thus cut down the time and effort in cleansing the body. Otherwise the job has to be done through meditation, involving time, effort and physical disorders.

When Chitvan, who is qualified in essential oils and herbs therapy, learnt of the problems I faced due to high levels of denseness, she recommended use of capsules made of herbs and essential oils. I tried them for a fortnight with dramatic results with quick, easy removal of denseness. Had I continued with the capsules, I am sure that I would have had a less traumatic time and faster progress.

However, I gave up the capsules after a fortnight as I felt that a quick-fix solution was not in consonance with my voluntary resolve to 'find' myself. I had myself created what was inside me and, therefore, I thought that I must go through the natural process of clearing it, no matter how long it took to complete the process and no matter what problems I faced. Moreover, in line with my thinking that much of spiritual development is a bio-spiritual phenomenon during at least the preliminary stage, I wanted to gain an understanding of how my system behaved or coped with the problems. I also thought, and I think rightly, that if the preliminary stage itself was so problematic and difficult to reach, the onward journey would impose and greater physical and mental strain and if so, I must prepare myself to be ready to face it.

***

I came to believe that the head top or the brain was the source, the production and dissemination centre of all denseness. I say this firstly because all the strands, one way or the other, originated from the head. Secondly, all, or substantially all, denseness moved to the head to disappear from there, except off and on and in the final stages when blocks of solid compartmentalised denseness were being cleared. In fact the cyclical character of denseness, that is to say originating from the head to percolate all over the body and travelling back to the head, its very source, to disintegrate there, is in conformity with Nature's law of everything being cyclical.

Denseness, I think, is a negative energy produced by unwholesome food and thoughts, emotions and actions. The two factors tend to cross-feed each other, each one nourishing the other with a view for each to strengthen its own position and role. It is only when the seed for spiritual awakening and development embedded within sprouts somehow that transformation starts to take place. The first step is disintegration of denseness as if without a trace in the body itself where it found its birth and straightening out of the off-course nerves. The second, and to some extent complementary or simultaneous activity, step is the conversion of negative energy into positive, subtle energy which brings about the transformation.

Disintegration of negative energy or its conversion into positive energy affects the body in various ways. Every serious practitioner of meditation experiences different kinds of physical occurrences and disorders for which there is no apparent or rational or as yet identified medical cause – the physical occurrences may be quite innocuous, such as humming sound in ears, watering and itching of eyes, itching sensation wherever denseness gets separated or peeled off from the skin, nose watering, etc. Or the occurrences may be minor or in the nature of a serious disorder such as discharge of mucus and phlegm, dull headaches and other aches and pains in different parts of the body, changes in digestive pattern, eruption of pimples and boils, changes in sleep pattern, etc. It is, therefore, obvious that denseness is a biological phenomenon of which one is not conscious in normal life. One becomes conscious of its existence and disintegration only when one begins to look deep within.

The fact is that medical science, be it allopathy, homeopathy or Ayurveda, is as yet an inexact and incomplete science. Firstly, it is not aware of denseness in the body and, therefore, has not investigated why and how it arises and what its effects are physically, emotionally, mentally or spiritually. Secondly, there are a number of diseases such as cataract, prostrate and arthritis, of which medical science has not been able to identify the exact cause. It is content to explain them away as occurring due to either age or to one's genes. Though not visible to the present-day scientific instruments, denseness does exist in the body. It is full of impurities because the disintegration of denseness does cause a variety of serious or insignificant disorders, of which there are no rational or scientific explanations. It is, therefore, probable that many of the diseases of which the cause is not yet known may be due to denseness and deflected nerves.

***

The human body has an, elaborate nervous system. There are three types of nerves in the body – sensory nerves that receive external stimulus and convert them into electrical impulses; adjustor nerves that select, interpret or modify the impulses from sensory nerves; and motor nerves that carry the modified impulses to the brain and bring back the brain's responses to the external stimuli for action by tissues and glands.

I discovered later, when I went through medical books, Section Three of the Strand System was substantially similar to one of the main sensory nerve pathways from the skin to the cerebrum. This leads me to believe that the rest of the Strand System too must also consist of sensory and motor nerves.

The brain has a 'massive complex of neural processing centres (pain, touch and possibly sound selection) that receive input from all systems, with the exception of olfactory system and are brought to consciousness' in the brain. A part of the brain also affects sleep cycle and state of contentment and well-being. Another part is 'somehow involved with such qualities as disposition, outlook on life, drive, personality, planning for the future and control of activities along ethical lines' (*Encyclopaedia Britannica*, volume 12).

Medical science says that arteries get coated with plaque due to cholesterol and other reasons. Arteries are also elastic and the extent of elastic movement or dilation depends on the structure of the surrounding tissues. Medical people I have met do not say anything as to whether the nerves too can get coated. They do, however, say that nerves are firm and cannot dilate. If arteries get coated, then it seems logical that nerves too can gather some sort of accumulation. In fact, they actually do, as I found that many of the thick nerves became thinner as denseness disintegrated. I also found that most of the nerves in the Strands System and others not mentioned in the Strands System had shifted their position and quite widely.

***

I was not conscious of denseness and nor of twisted nerves until I started looking within. In other words, there was another dimension of the body that revealed itself when I started looking within. I believe that the human physical system has two main compartments – the outer or the upper, and the inner or the deeper. Most spiritual philosophers describe what I call the 'deeper' as 'subtle' or 'astral' body and diagrammatically depict it as being above the outer body. As I experienced, the second physical system exists inside the body itself; I call it the inner or the deeper physical. The two compartments are closely interlinked, with constant interaction, without a clear-cut line of demarcation and have a considerable overlap in functions and responses.

I subdivide each of the two compartments further into two parts – the upper into physical and physical-spiritual, and the deeper into spiritual-physical and spiritual. The difference between the physical-spiritual and the spiritual-physical is that the former is more physically active and less active spiritually and the latter is the other way around. I describe these four as Physical, Bio-Spiritual, Spiritual-Physical and Spiritual.

My experience so far is limited to the Bio-Spiritual and it appears to me that the next stage would have greater spiritual content till the eventual stage when nothing will exist except the self.

The two compartments, Physical and Bio-Spiritual, share the physical framework with two significant differences. The first difference was that the Physical has all the organs and nerves, veins, arteries, etc. The Bio-Spiritual comprises the body-frame, denseness and nerves – there is nothing else in it; it is boneless and I think there are no arteries of even veins. Nerves are an essential component as in addition to the physical function of being the carriers of sensations and responses to/from the brain, they also carry spiritual or subtle energy and disperse it in the whole system through their vast network. In fact, the Bio-Spiritual is mainly concerned with spiritual development. It has, therefore, no need of bones, muscles, arteries or veins.

When I experienced the shafts of denseness rise from the region below the lower end of the spinal cord and press the upper body, there were no obstructions. The shafts and occasionally other strong vibrations would literally squash a particular area down, rendering it completely out of shape as if it was made of jelly or clay. There were no obstructive bones, muscles, arteries or veins in the way.

The second difference was that whilst the upper or the physical body utilised the physical structure for physical, emotional and mental development and other purposes, the inner one utilises it for deeper, wider and more significant function of spiritual development and to bring about a transformation in thoughts, actions and sense of values.

The Physical and the Bio-Spiritual actively interact with each other. In many ways, one is the shadow of the other; what happens in one has a deep impact on the other. Physical actions, emotions or thoughts and the type of food one imbibes create a deep impact on the Bio-Spiritual through production of denseness that, in turn, affects the nerves and the quality of thoughts, emotions, actions and spiritual development. After the Bio-Spiritual opens up, it begins to holistically purify the physical, getting rid of physical toxicity through various types of disorders and to radically transform the physical, thoughts, emotions and actions, injecting a new quality of life.

***

During the final stages, I found that all the nerves in the Strands System and many others were hooked to other nerves at more than one place. Some of the nerves were sharply bent. The inner body bore no resemblance to normal physical body. The whole inner body was in a slouching position. The throat and the upper portion, from the middle of the ears to the top of the head, were tightly compressed as if the areas had been sealed off to make them inaccessible. The upper chest and the area from the thighs downward right up to the feet, had been pushed forward. The area from the lower chest to the buttocks seemingly remained in position but was in fact pushed back.

All the nerves on the left side had been pushed upward by thick layers of extremely tough, rubber-like denseness that would become tight under pressure. It would thin down and disperse over the rest of the body only after three or four meditation sessions. The right-side nerves had moved downward, submerged under thick, solidified denseness. The inner structure was a rickety structure, wavy and zigzag, and imbalanced with left side higher than the right side. It was held together by numerous rings and tight junctions.

To make matters worse, two thin masses of nerves covering the upper part of the body were compressed together, hooked to each other all over, on the sides and in the middle, right from the top of the head down to below the hips. A thin nerves-mass in the back was literally sewn up to the body at the shoulder blade and pelvis.

The inner self was buried and buried deep, as if in a strong custom-made coffin, bolted by multiple junctions and tied around by wire-like rings all over the body. It was nothing short of a miracle that the inner self could break loose to resurrect to bestow a new, meaningful life.

Had the inner self been visible to physical eyes, it would have looked as ugly, disfigured and ghastly as the painting of Dorian Gray looked eventually in the novel *The Picture of Dorian Gray* by Oscar Wilde. Though Dorian Gray continued to look healthy and handsome outwardly, the painting changed every time he committed an unwholesome or heinous act. The painting represented Dorian Gray's inner self that bore the pangs and sorrows of his deeds and depicted his true self that bore no resemblance to the outer, visible appearance.

***

Even though I started meditation in 1993-94, I did not become conscious of denseness till August 2000 and it was only in October 2000 that I began to feel the pressure of constant forceful movement of vibrations resulting in sleeplessness and inability to concentrate.

For a considerable time, I thought, that frequent changes in my meditation technique were probably the cause of the unusual developments. Though frequent changes in technique might have prolonged the process of clearance of denseness, I never believed that it were the twisted, off-course nerves that ware responsible for the peculiar development. It seems to me that I must have gained entry into the Bio-Spiritual in October 1999 when the deflated nerves, uprooted from their long-held unnatural position, began to pulsate under the impact of vibrations during meditation and otherwise, were straining to get back to their lost position. When any of the nerves was restored to its natural position, it ceased to pulsate.

For a long time I thought that it was the Force that had triggered of the non-stop vibrations. I now believe that it was only a natural phenomenon of the Bio-Spiritual and that the vibrations set in motion by breathing led to constant pulsation of homeless, displaced nerves, eager get back to their natural, or the subsequent long-held position.

The question is to what extent the cleansing of the body and of the nerves of denseness and restoration of the topsy-turvy nervous system to its normal position was responsible for the change in my perceptions, values and way of life. Were these two factors entirely responsible for the change? I think that the removal of denseness resulted in removing the impurities in the physical body and that, in turn, had some impact on my thinking and emotional responses. This was an important first step as a clean body and a clean mind do go hand-in-hand.

Science believes that the nervous system is 'somehow' involved with one's outlook of life, overall life style and sense of values. Science concerns itself with changes that are visible and can be objectively verified. Science is not concerned with inner or spiritual development and in this context does not recognise the existence of an inner body or what I call the Bio-Spiritual. However, having observed deflected nerves in the inner body and their gradual straightening out, I believe that the radical change in my sense of values and attitude towards life is connected with the restoration of damaged nerves in the Bio-Spiritual to normal functioning.

At the same time, the fact is that I began to change and had changed somewhat before I became conscious of the denseness and its removal and of deflected nerves and their straightening out. The changes were not ordinary changes. Besides cleansing the body of impurities, the other changes were extraordinary changes. For example, I became a vegetarian and a teetotaller and began to develop belief in God. I used to feel sudden joy and flows of subtle vibration that would fill up my whole body with a soothing sense of well-being and self-assurance. I also had a number of unusual experiences, described later, of receiving messages, more or less like directives, from an anonymous, objectively unidentifiable voice. These and some other changes were all the more extraordinary as they were not willed or planned by me. They just came about. In other words, the removal of denseness and normal functioning of the inner nervous system could not by themselves have been the transforming agencies. There was some other entity that was responsible for the changes. This entity, I believe, was the Force.

A relevant question is, what is it that led to the awakening of the Force? I think it was two probable, interconnected reasons. Firstly, I started to seriously look at my entire past, minutely and critically examining all the significant happenings. The process, rightly or wrongly, led me to the conclusion that the past life had been an utter waste. Secondly, I made a firm resolve that I would change my way of life. Slowly, I developed the habit of examining every thought, feeling and emotion as it arose and made an earnest effort to shut out the ones that I considered unwanted or undesirable. When I decided to change my way of life, I did not chart out what I wanted or what the new way of life should be. All the changes came about automatically, The pattern and type of changes, I think, were already 'written', as religion says.

***

Straightening out of deflected nerves was a Herculean task, the toughest, single task ever in my life. These nerves were embedded in a hard layer-after-layer of denseness, mostly in the back, held down by five or six rings below the pelvis, neck and the head and by at least six tough junctions of multiple nerves on each side of the body. The main nerves and the rings were hooked with minor nerves at numerous places. The nerves in the junctions broke loose only when they were reverted, more or less, to their natural path. The entire process of restoring nerves to their normal position took more than six months.

The disintegration of hard denseness and disentanglement of junction nerves led to generation of excessive heat in the body all through the long, six month period. I was perforce obliged to give up tea and coffee and even mildly spicy or chilly-hot food. I would drink 8–10 glasses of cold nimboo-pani during the day, have large bowls of cold curd before every meal including breakfast and had to resort to fruit for breakfast and soup and salad or steamed vegetables for lunch. I did however, take normal but non-spicy food for dinner.

The displaced nerves caused two other physical problems, more serious than any experienced earlier. Firstly, the deflected nerves, in combination with heavy, viscous denseness in the area below the base of spinal cord blocked the passage of stools. One or the other passage for passing would partially open due clearance of denseness or shifting of deflected nerves. The large intake of water every morning on empty stomach helped as water exerted forceful pressure on the abdomen. By and large, I remained partially constipated for a considerable time.

Secondly, as the head or the brain where nerves originated had been firmly compressed, most of the nerves had deflected in the brain itself. The deflected nerves would constantly pulsate, resulting in high blood pressure.

I discussed the two developments with Sraddhalu. He suggested that I do yoga asanas twice a day instead of just once, followed by two breathing exercises – first one, inhale through one nostril, hold breath for a little while and exhale from the second nostril; then inhale through the second nostril and exhale from the first nostril and repeat the process a number of times and second one, breathe in through both nostrils simultaneously, hold breath for a while and breathe out through both the nostrils. The two suggestions were a great help in clearing up denseness.

With regard to the problem of blood pressure, Sraddhalu said that whenever I had a heavy head or felt that I had blood pressure, I should concentrate on the head. I found the device extremely effective.

Sraddhalu also asked me to change the meditation technique. Instead of meditating on the heart-centre, I should concentrate an inch or so above the heart-centre. This place is the meeting point of the two cross-way nerves in Section Two and the nerve above the spinal cord referred in Section Six. The change in techniques, he said, would hasten the opening up of the psyche. The new technique made sense. The new spot is strategically located; it is in the middle of the spinal cord on which all the chakras are located. Moreover, the spot is the meeting point of two major sensory nerves and the nerve above the spine, and all three together have an extensive reach, up and down and sideways.

***

Most writers on meditation prescribe a long list of pre-requisites for success. These include wholesome, moralistic life; self-denial; detachment; avoidance of alcohol; simple, non-spicy, vegetarian food; etc. I had plunged into meditation without any preparation, with the sole objective of finding out more about myself and, if possible, my true self. At that time, I did all that was forbidden by the meditation gurus. Later, I confronted serious problems for which I could get no explanation or solution from others. By the time I met Sraddhalu, I had already experienced remarkable changes in my attitude towards life and behaviour, occasional unaccountable joy and a feeling of well-being. I already used to spend considerable time in looking within, so much so that I was left with less and less time and inclination to pay attention to external matters, leading to a general sense of detachment. I had also found that my body preferred simple food, declining to accept any non-vegetarian or spicy food or alcohol.

Gradually I had developed my own list of essential and nonessentials, of do's and don'ts. The do's and don'ts later led to the development of what I call a 'cultivated' code of thoughts and conduct. I call it 'cultivated' because it was a put-together code, needing effort and constant vigil to guard against deviations and tendency to relapse into the old self and its old ways. I am still in that stage. However, I think that over time the cultivated code will get distilled and purified, culminating into a 'Law of the Self' – permanent spontaneous expression hopefully of an integrated personality.

***

The spiritual community says that it is imperative to have a guru to learn meditation and to progress in its pursuit. According to me, a guru implies someone in whom one reposes implicit faith and surrenders totally to the guru. The institution of guru was set up in olden times in India when people lived simple and values-based life. They lived in small communities and there were a limited number of well-known and recognised spiritualists who had done long years of tapasya (penance) and truly earned the status of a guru. The guru was not just a teacher of yoga and meditation; the guru was a philosopher and guide on all matters, personal, spiritual or social.

These are different times. The day-to-day life is full of constant stress and strains and millions and millions of people all over the world are taking to meditation and spiritualism to seek respite from the fast pace of life. Most of them look for a guru in the hope of learning the kind of meditation that can quickly lessen the burden of frustration on them and deliver some peace of mind.

At the same time, there is a proliferation of self-styled swamis and yogis and a multitude of institutions for the purpose of teaching meditation. For most, meditation or spiritualism is a business venture.

During my limited interaction with individual swamis and teachers in spiritual institutions, I found that some of them lacked sensitivity; most of them did not have sufficient or deep knowledge of the problems that a meditator might come across; some were rather supercilious, treating learners as inferior or at best a class below as uniformed lay persons; some, adept in human psychology, would promise fast, attractive and misleading results in accordance with the learner's desires and expectations. Most of them would offer explanations in symbolic terms that would leave the learner more confused than before. As the seekers of peace of mind are willing to pay generously, meditation and spiritualism, like religion, have become a lucrative business with rampant exploitation.

Exploitation of need for inner peace and development is the worst form of exploitation. It is exploitation of inner aspiration, unlike that of other kinds of needs and ambitions that mostly pertain to material aspects of life. There is a strong need for a code of conduct amongst swamis and spiritual teachers, like the code of conduct evolved by associations of medical practitioners, charted accountants and other bodies.

The objective of meditation is inner development and each person 'inside' is unique, being the product of a multitude of diverse factors. It is, therefore, impossible to predict into what form an 'inside' will unravel, except in rather general terms. As such, how much or what type of guidance can another person provide is a moot point.

I found that the 'inside' itself is the guru. I set out on the path on my own, compelled to do so by an inner urge. Beside some very valuable, occasional advice from Sraddhalu, it was predominantly the Force that guided me thorough the tortuous journey to complete the preliminary stage. It gave me insight into many inner occurrences and developments, clarified doubts and uncertainties and lifted me out of spells of depression, whenever required.

There is another aspect to the complex subject of meditation. Meditation, in fact, is all about transformation of the self. The inner changes that take place are both positive and negative. I went through nervous bouts of doubts, dismay and depression at the frustratingly slow, tedious progress and strange, inexplicable developments. Time and again, I felt a desperate need to discuss the strange happenings with someone and yearned for reassurance that all was well and there was no physical, emotional or mental risk. It was, therefore, necessary to find someone knowledgeable, sensitive and personally experienced with whom I could talk about the happenings inside me and seek advice. I consider such a person as a consultant. Sraddhalu, who provided valuable support and helped me build confidence, himself demurred at being called a guru.

***

I first thought that it was the Force that cleaned the denseness. Later I noticed that clearance of denseness was, to a considerable extent, an automatic phenomenon. I now think that whilst denseness gets automatically cleared during single-spot meditation and by deflected nerves straining to resumes their natural pathways during other times, the Force played a crucial part in clearing denseness in two ways.

I noted earlier that shafts of thick, viscous denseness arose from the region from the base of the spine to the lower buttock. Initially, I disliked the development as I thought that the shafts were responsible for spreading sticky thickness in other parts of the body and thus increase the number of difficult areas already there. Subsequently, I realised that I was wrong. I found that these shafts played a supportive role to the Force in clearing and straightening out the off-course nerves. The Force emanating from the brain cleared denseness and worked on deflected nerves during roving mediation. The shafts performed the same job during single spot mediation. The shafts would rise and move to an area where there was actual or partial difficulty. While the Force would generally soften the area and also clear denseness, the shafts would only soften the spot through firm and often quite rough pressure. It was obvious that the Force that arose from the brain and shafts that arose from the area below the base of the spine worked in tandem in view of the complementary role of shafts. I called them Force II.

There were other differences between the Force and Force II. Unlike Force II, the Force was hardly ever aggressive – it mostly worked softly. Usually the Force moved from one nerve to an interconnecting nerve, cleared difficult spots on the way and moved to another connecting nerve and so on. The Force, thus, had an unrestricted range.

Unlike that, Force II worked only through forceful pressure and aggressively. The Force was more resourceful and deployed different means depending on the situation. In sensitive areas, it would work very gently with scalpel-like fine and thin tools. In areas of thick denseness, it would exert firm pressure. Often it would split itself into two or create an assistant to tackle the area.

The activity of Force II was restricted only to clearance of denseness and straightening out of twisted nerves. The Force had a comprehensive wide-ranging role. I credit the Force for opening up the Bio-Spiritual body and for bringing about a transformation in my outlook and way of life.

The Force was indestructible. In the early stages, during the time I attended the second Vipassana course, it would move in the shape of a small, longish, jelly-like piece. I was curious to find out what it was and once I managed to hold it in between my teeth. I pressed, the place hard for a minute or so. The piece vibrated like jelly and did not disintegrate. The Force moved in the form of a small piece only in the beginning. Later, it became a formless energy.

The Force possessed other attributes like human beings. It had a memory; it would resume unfinished work in clearing denseness from an earlier session. It was considerate; it handled sensitive parts softly and with care so as not to cause damage. It was resourceful; it used different methods and implements to tackle different parts.

Above all, the Force was a benevolent and conscious entity with spiritual powers. It listened and responded to my prayer to let me sleep as I mentioned earlier.

From 1993 onwards, when I started to look within, I had some unusual experiences. I would at this stage note down only one kind of messages received from within. The messages had a direct bearing on the inner revolution.

It is more than likely that everyone receives messages in the ordinary course of life and that I too must have received them earlier. Maybe one calls them, hunches. In the case of some, most of the hunches come right. These must be in respect of people who, consciously or unconsciously, have well developed inner selves. In other cases, as in my own, most of the hunches were incorrect. I used to treat my hunches that came true as intelligent guesses and the ones that proved false as products of wishful thinking.

The Force

The messages that I got from 1993 were not a matter of feeling, as hunches often are. It was always a voice that delivered the message, a short, crisp message, almost like a command. It was an unidentifiable voice, a voice that was, in fact, voiceless or to use the title of a short book by Madame Blavatsky, 'the voice of silence'. All the messages had a uniform style, a few words delivered as a command and always much before dawn, around 3.30 or 4 a.m. Every single message pertained to some mental doubt or concern and suggested the way out.

In October 1993, I decided to visit Dubai where I was earlier working with a company that eventually got into serious financial problems and collapsed with large debts. Consequently, one of its main directors was put behind bars. I had some of my baggage lying in Dubai and I decided to go there to get it and also complete some pending work. One early morning, something from within said, 'Don't go to Dubai.' I did not go and was able to handle the outstanding matters by phone and letters. Had I gone to Dubai, I would perhaps have invited adverse action either from Dubai authorities or the erstwhile management of the company I worked for.

I was in Nainital in September 1997. Looking at the mountains, I developed a strong urge to give up my consultancy work. I did not pay heed to the feeling and continued to strain hard and took a number of initiatives to get some assignments. I was also approached by some people to submit proposals. However, neither my initiatives nor the approaches of other people fructified I was greatly concerned at the development and wondered for days about what to do. One morning in late 1998, the voice said, 'Keep on looking within,' The die was cast and I closed my consultancy business.

Sometime in 1998, the voice said, 'The whole world is within you. It does not exist outside.' It then dawned on me that all things and all people are, in fact, as I saw them.

The moon as I saw was one thing to me, another to a poet and yet another to an astronomer. Similarly, a person to me was one type, and to himself or herself may be another type and to a third person, yet another. I had read often that the world was within oneself. But that morning this realisation came like a bolt of lightning, clear and luminous. I felt excited as if I had discovered something new, that was never known earlier!

There were two more remarkable experience of a different kind. On 19 February 1994, on the eve of my birthday, I sat in front of the TV with a drink in my hand. All of a sudden, without any such thought either then or ever earlier, I made a statement, of course silently, that I dedicated all that was mine to you. The statement shook me in pleasant manner. The amazing thing was that there was no cause, no provocation, and no inducement. The statement came out without thought, totally spontaneous and from the depths of my heart.

I have not yet fulfilled the commitment. If at all, it remains only partially fulfilled. Leave aside material possessions, my surrender in thought and in deed is not a total surrender. I have to go a long way.

The second experience also took place in 1994. I had gone for a walk. All of a sudden, as much without forethought and as spontaneously as the previous incident, I said 'Try me out with any adversity.' Later, whenever I felt fed up or frustrated – and there have been numerous such occasions including the huge number of problems and prolonged delay in clearing of denseness and straightening out of nerves – I am always reminded of the promise I made, that too, entirely voluntarily.

24 July 2002

The Journey Continues

The last decade, since 1993 when I set out on the path of finding myself, two time periods stand out as the most significant – the first, the year 1994 and the second, the period from August 2001 to October 2002.

The first period was marked by subtle, delightful sensations, frequent feeling of joy, meaningful thought and experiences that laid the foundations of my commitment to the new path and of my present thinking or philosophy. The second period was marked by a sense of quietness and peace, removal of many of the earlier doubts and confusions, and a deeper commitment to the pursuit of finding self – that became the sole objective of my life. At the same time, the second period was a difficult, tumultuous period, dominated by an obsession to see the end of physical cleansing and rectification of the damaged, chaotic, inner nervous system. There was a near absence of subtle sensations, infrequent sense of joy and relatively few new thoughts. I was so much involved with the task restoration of nerves to their natural pathways and the resulting problems that even if there were any subtle sensations, I did not notice them. Obsession with denseness and the nerves was, in fact, largely involuntary because of the highly excessive denseness and constant irritating vibrations of displaced and deflected nerves straining to regain their natural position, leaving no scope for anything else.

The first time I experienced an unusually delightful and a very special feeling was in March 1994 – a calm, blank, deep inner void, utter silence, muted gentle breath and the area from the crown to the upper back as one integrated and sensuously warm mass. Soon the warmth permeated the whole body, giving rise to the feeling that the body was on an air-cushion, in fact, actually floating in the air. The combined experience of an integrated body and the body floating in the air has never repeated itself.

As I mentioned earlier, I used to concentrate on the middle of the eyebrows in mid-1994. I would occasionally see a yellow spot, shaped like a fish, in the middle of the brow. At times the spot would become bigger and appear as a shapeless mass. A dark grey patch would often replace the yellow spot. At other times, a red spot, more of flame colour, would mix with yellow and be there over the entire brow, giving a feeling that the grey band of colours was without a border or limit. At one time, yellow was replaced by luminous white and I found my lower lip and a part of the chin shaking involuntarily. Like a fool, I began to pay attention to the shaking lip and chin. That stopped the shaking, but simultaneously, the coloured patch disappeared. Later, I regretted having diverted my attention from the middle of the brow and felt that I should have kept on concentrating on the luminous white.

The sense of joy was an occasional experience that occurred mostly during meditation and often lingered on for a considerable time. No sensuous pleasure of any type had ever been so fulfilling. The unique thing was that the joy was simple in essence, not dependent on anything external, just being with self, all by myself in meditation,

The Journey Continues

yet beyond myself, in emptiness, a fulfilling, satisfying emptiness – no memory, no dream and no sense of future.

In 1994, I would feel an indescribable feeling of something surging within, up and down, in the back and in the front, exerting gentle pressure sometime and, other times, giving the feeling that the waves would burst out of the body. At these times, there would be a gentle pressure on the face, eyes in particular, pressing the eyelids down and down, closing them tighter and tighter. Despite all the pressure, there would be no ache or pain or discomfort; it would be just a pure and delightful pressure.

I often wondered – What was it that surged up and down? Was it energy? If so, why did the energy start to flow during meditation? Was it that when one stopped to think, only then did the energy flow? Or was it that when we think, we consume energy and that is why there are no vibrations? Or is it, and which was most likely, that it was only when the mind was still that we observed the flow of energy? And what kind of energy was it ? It was certainly not physical energy.

It was a period of growing quietude, with a greater and greater feeling of 'letting things be', a feeling that heavens won't fall if things did not happen as per plan. However, I found that it was easy to decide to let things be, just 'be' rather than 'become', and extremely difficult actually to detach myself from the goings-on. All my life I had been making efforts 'become'. 'Being' meant to live effortlessly. I found that, in fact, living effortlessly required much greater effort than effortful life.

The feeling of peace within would come and go, taken over by moods of depression and frustration with the past way of life. In earlier times, the dominant life objective was personal achievement through hard work and a passion to keep the mind engaged in thoughts, mostly job-related thoughts. I strongly believed in the popular saying that an idle mind is the devil's workshop. I considered mind as a God that was the key to success, constantly endeavouring to make it sharper and sharper, more and more analytical and resourceful to conceive new work-related plans. At the end of a hard day's work, I would drown myself in wining and dining, as a method of seeking relief and a well-earned compensation for a hard day's labour.

It is, in a sense, ironical that I began to consider the same mind that I earlier looked at as the architect of success, as a villain of the piece and that it must be muted and set aside. However, the effort to silence the mind was restricted to the duration of meditation only and not otherwise as a general habit. It is obvious that the fixed idea of long hours of hard work and evening merry-making was an escape from the inner dissatisfaction with the way I lived my life. The bubble had to burst – as it did and just as well.

A contributory reason for the feeling of frustration and depression was the secluded, inactive life that I led at that time. I recognised that I needed to be active. Yet, because of growing quietude and occasional feeling of joy, I thought that looking or living within was better than living in the outside world. As such, I would often think, why should I not retire and sit peacefully? This, in a way, would not be an escape from life. After all, externalism was an escape from facing the self and from coming to terms with it. Similarly, looking and living within would be an escape from the external world, which, I thought, was a harsh reality despite many moments of relief and cognizable benefits in the outside world. The confusion got resolved in course of time.

***

I would often feel very sad. The feeling of sadness would descend suddenly even after the whole day had gone off well. I would feel as if everything was coming apart. There was so much aloneness, living in a world peopled only by myself. I would usually feel being in a peculiar state. I would want to wish for something but would not be able to put my finger on what actually I could wish. I was in a stagnant situation. I would wonder what the end would be, how long the period of sadness and depression would go on, and how long I would remain in the position of not knowing what I wanted. And then I would ask myself as to why I wanted to know how long. Could anyone forecast the length of future?

In fact, I secretly hoped that an answer, an assurance that there would be an end to loneliness at some particular point of time would come from somewhere within. I would fruitlessly tell myself that the answer lay within and that when the within was weak or hollow, doubts and dismay were bound to creep in. I realised that I had to learn to cope with myself.

I would tell myself that I had little choice but to go on with my aloneness and continue to let things be. At the same time, I would wonder whether letting life be was like living like a vegetable, just growing and then reaching decay, without will and volition. I would I helplessly end the discussion with myself with the short answer that I did not know the answer.

I started to do professional work once again and enjoyed it immensely. It was the type of work that suited my approach to life at that time, working on my own as a consultant, doing research and writing articles. I felt that writing articles was fun – fun because if one wrote something that made sense, one felt that one had done something distinctive. People called it making a contribution. It was fun also because one got noticed and talked about and that pleased the ego. That's it, the ego. Was the word 'ego' a dirty word? Suppose one was to say that it pleased the 'self', would that make difference? Would that change the situation? So, I would think that it was all a matter of words. In my dictionary of the time, self was superior to ego.

Ego, in fact, is, I thought and think, a complex subject. After I started meditation, I tried to submerge the ego. After a few years, I noticed the emergence of ego in a different form, sublimated, so to say, into sense of dignity and self-respect. Whenever I felt that I had been wronged, I felt a forceful surge of anger and would strongly react, and react emotionally. And that, I thought, was not what I had set out to achieve through meditation. I decided to become more circumspect and watchful of my feelings of being wronged. Did I feel bad because my sense of pride was hurt or was it that the happening really violated my sense of values and that too my sense of personal values? I succeeded in controlling my reactions. However, I realise that the solution was a makeshift solution; a controlled or submerged ego is not the same as wiped out or extinct ego. I still have a long way to go!

I enjoyed the work also because it allowed considerable free time to meditate and look within. I found that looking within, analysing all thoughts, emotions and actions, produced amazing results, slowly but surely.

I began to believe that all relationships were motivated by self-interest. Pursuing the thought further, I would wonder – was it simply that all the happenings were an outcome of one's own self-interest or was it that the happenings were an outcome of interaction of the self with others' self-interests or selves? I thought that if something occurred contrary to expectations, was it not that someone else's will or self-interest was stronger than one's own? Was it right to assume that what had happened had been ordained? And I would wonder whether it was valid to think that the ordinary course of life was predetermined. I still think that neither all the ordinary nor, in fact, each and every extraordinary event of life is precisely predetermined. There is an element, and a strong one, of free will. The predetermination is there but rather in very broad terms.

The Journey Continues

Resolutions, I thought, including birthday resolutions, were meaningless. What should one resolve to do when one could not often clearly distinguish between right and wrong? Moreover, as resolutions relate to bringing some change – change in habits, traits, attitude or behaviour – a resolution to change meant suppression of what one thought was undesirable. Suppression is counter-productive, it cannot bring about positive or desired results. Besides, it creates unnecessary tension in the mind. What is needed is an organic transformation, a change that springs or flows from within. One should just be – be what one is. The only resolution I thought one could make was to find out what who one is and what 'being' really means. And pursue wilfully the path charted out as the 'being' path. In any case, I thought and continue to think that every day is a new day, as special as any other. And when the main resolve has already been made to 'be', what is the purpose of making it again or another one?

I also developed a dislike for the concept of duty. I thought that it was an unnatural concept, as it imposed a sense of obligation – obligation to do something or to behave in particular ways that one may not actually like or want to. The whole structure of duties – being a good father, husband or son, a good citizen and so on rested on the philosophy of 'becoming'. Why the obligation and imposition of a requirement that did not find an inner accord? And if one did what was expected out of compulsion, would the outcome not be negative or at best non-positive? I still do not like the concept of 'duty'.

Instead, if one were to learn just to 'be', would one be a bad father, husband or son or a bad citizen? After all, I had not charted the path of change in life. There is a law of Nature and the changes occurred in accordance with that law. The fact that many of the changes that have occurred are on the lines of a long list of prerequisites prescribed by the gurus and religious orders underlines the contention that personal changes need not normally be imposed through pressure or persuasion. The only change needed is the change to learn to look within and endeavour to lead an inner life.

I gradually developed a sense of detachment and found that detachment from the past automatically grew into detachment from the present because the present, for most of us, is nothing but the past and some bits of thoughts about the future.

In late August 1994, around 4 a.m., a sudden thought or rather a voice said, 'Have faith in yourself and God.' As I have mentioned earlier about the other messages, this message too carried a tremendous force. Over a period of time, the strength of the force diminished, clouded by a sense of unreality – a feeling that the message was not that significant or unusual. Yet when the message came, and it came out of nothing, out of nowhere, it got firmly imprinted in my mind unlike other thoughts.

In an unusual book *Conversations with God*, Neale Donald Walsh terms experiences during meditation as being revealed to a person as 'a personal epiphany'. He goes on to say, 'Once you have had such a magnificent experience, it can be very difficult to go back to "real life" in a way that blends well with what other people are calling "reality". That is because your reality has shifted . . . It has expanded, grown.' (Book 3).

In the same book, Walsh says, 'You are at choice, always, about what you wish to experience. . . . The soul responds to, recreates, the mind's most powerful suggestion, producing that in its experience. . . . (Some) souls quickly adjust, see the experience for what it is, begin to think new thought, and move immediately to new experiences.'

I think that Walsh makes a lot of sense. All the messages that I received were in the context of the situations that I faced; and all the messages offered solutions to the problems

The Journey Continues

at hand. Would it be, then, that all the solutions conveyed by the messages were, in fact, there in my inner thoughts that I was not conscious of? A significant difference, however, between thoughts and messages was that the messages were not thoughts – they were commands.

In the previous chapter, I mentioned two other experiences I had in 1994 which were in the nature of thoughts or pronouncements – first, dedicating all to Him and the second asking Him to try me out with any type of adversity. I think both were pronouncements of what I had read somewhere that had sunk indelibly in my subconscious as what I needed to do.

The experience, when one early morning on one day in 1998, I heard the voice say, 'The whole world is within you' was, I think, a flash of insight and that is why the thought, an ordinary and a very common one, came with a tremendous force to make a lasting impact. Eckhart Tolle in *The Power of Now* says that Zen masters describe a flash as 'satori', 'a moment of no-mind and total presence'. He also says that 'although satori is not a lasting transformation . . . it gives you a taste of enlightenment'. He calls the state in which flashes occur as 'presence', that is, 'something ineffable, some deep, inner, holy essence' for which total quietness of mind is a must and that was exactly the situation when I heard the voice.

I received all the messages in the early hours of the morning when the mind was totally quiet after night's sleep and in a state of total 'presence'. That is also the reason why the meditation gurus say that the best time for meditation is early morning.

Almost all the auditory experiences took place in 1994. The power and force of the experiences, in fact, determined the unwavering and steadfast resolve to pursue the new course for the rest of my life. It is remarkable that there were no auditory experiences, no messages, and no commands after 1994. Is it that they were needed in the initial stages to show and demarcate the path and, through being firmly and indelibly rooted in the mind, the experiences were to serve as a beacon to dispel doubts and confusion whenever they would arise, as also to ensure unwavering pursuit of the assigned path? Or is it that commands, as such, are needed only in the beginning stages, to compel a certain type of person, particularly dominantly egoistic type, to follow a certain way of life? And when the inner consciousness begins to take roots, the Force considers the stratagem of 'obedience' as unnecessary, and replaces it by guidance imparted in the form of inner or intuitive thoughts and voluntary volition?

***

When I finished writing the previous chapter on 24 July 2002, I thought that it would take another week or so to complete the first stage. Instead, it took nearly 12 weeks to do so, proving that, as many a time earlier I was not capable of forecasting what laid ahead. There were still many pockets of denseness and numerous junctions. All the main nerves were off course by wide margins. Most of the nerves on the right side and in the area below the pelvis were hooked up with smaller, thinner nerves. There were still layers and layers of denseness, almost all in the back, with the entire Strands System and a few others that became noticeable later, and all the junctions still intact Additionally, the left side was permeated with thick, marshy denseness, stuck to the nerves, proving wrong the earlier impression that the left had less of denseness than the right side.

There were other noteworthy reasons for delayed completion of the first stage. At one time I had thought that there were ten nerve-loops from the top of the head down to the base of the spine. At the very end of the first stage, it seemed that there were in fact 12 loops and

The Journey Continues

the other was just straight nerves. I also observed at that stage that there were other main nerves over and above the nerves mentioned in the Strands System.

The most significant finding was the very large number of layers at the back. Each layer, particularly deeper down, has, I think, its own characteristics or complexities in terms of the type of denseness and distinctive pockets of denseness, or other special features relating to deflected or damaged nerves. In other words, the larger the number of layers, the bigger, more complex and more prolonged the ordeal to clean up and purify the Bio-Spiritual body.

Sri Aurobindo calls layers 'dense veils of in conscience' (*Synthesis of Yoga*). That means the removal of denseness does not only lead to physical purification but also mental and emotional cleansing and, as such, removal of denseness was the main cause of change in my sense of values and way of life.

All the nerves, loops or others, were intertwined with either other major or thin nerves. Contrary to what I felt and wrote earlier, I found that there were two thin-nerves masses, one at the back and the other in the front, and these extended from the topmost loop in the head to the lowest one at the base of the spine. The nerve-masses were stuck to each one of the loops; the toughest ones were the one around the neck and the other the pelvis loop. Additionally, the nerves-masses were stuck to other nerves on both the right and left sides.

In the monograph *The Chakras*, C.W. Leadbeater states that human beings have three bodies: physical, etheric and astral. Only the gross physical is visible to the eye; the other two – the etheric and the subtle or astral – are invisible. The etheric body is a form of 'faintly-luminous violet-grey mist' that interpenetrates the dense, physical body, and extends very slightly beyond it. It is a crucial instrument for the flow of vital energy into the body that is responsible for keeping us alive. It is also significantly the link for the flow of thoughts and feelings that are obviously spiritual in nature and content, from the astral to the physical body.

According to Leadbeater, there is an etheric web between the etheric and the astral bodies 'interpenetrating them in a manner not readily describable, (is) a sheath or web of closely woven texture, a sheath of single layer of physical atoms much compressed and permeated by a special type of vital force.' It is through the etheric web through which Divine life comes from the astral into the physical body. The etheric body also plays the important role of a natural shield to prevent a premature opening up of communication between the two planes – a development which could lead to nothing but injury.

Leadbeater expresses the view that narcotics and alcohol (as also tea and coffee) contain certain ingredients that pass from the physical to the astral body and, in the process, damage, and could eventually, destroy the etheric web. Destruction of the web could lead to 'brutality and animalism' and lesser damage of 'general deadening down of the man's qualities, resulting in gross materialism . . . the loss of all finer feelings through ossification of the web.'

Leadbeater's findings, based on personal experiences and 'careful observation of a number of Western students' led me to an important thought. Could it be that the two thin-nerves masses that I observed at the back and in the front and that appeared sewed up or glued up together on the sides and to all the major loops and main nerves were, in fact, the etheric web that, through large intake of alcohol over a long drinking career, got ossified and got stuck to the nerves in the inner body?

I mentioned in the previous chapter that it seemed to me as if the area above the neck had been sealed off because of excessive denseness in the neck. I noticed in the final

The Journey Continues

stage that it was a correct observation. The neck occupies a pivotal position for an erect posture. The neck in my inner body was a solid mass of denseness that covered the entire back portion of the head. No wonder that my inner body was a misshapen body with a deep slouch.

There are thousands of nerves in the body. As all main nerves in my body were deflected, consequently, their tributary nerves, too, were deflected. I also had a countless number of layers of denseness. Every time a layer got cleared, there followed a massive readjustment or relocation of nerves, with those nerves that had regained their natural pathways falling off and becoming invisible. As a combined effect of the vast number of deflected nerves and numerous layers, the last stages took a long, long time to get over.

The process of purification of the body continued till the very end, particularly by the way of discharge of mucus through the nose, watering of eyes and eruption of small boils inside the left side of the mouth.

I noticed another remarkable feature in the last and final stage. The left side was, by and large, a replica of the right side and the upper part of the body – from the upper chest to the crown and the lower part from the pelvis down to the base of the spine in terms of overall denseness and the number of junctions. However, one difference was in the quality or texture of denseness between the right and the left sides and between the upper and the lower parts. Another difference was that the head being the centrifugal point of nerves, was a more complex area than the lower parts.

I could not, in the final stages, meditate for more than an hour or so at a stretch, except in the early hours of the morning. In fact, I found that it was useful to meditate for short periods, with intervening gaps of 2 to 3 hours; physical movements during the intervals would soften the deflected nerves and the surrounding areas, making the sessions easier and less tortuous.

Sraddhalu had suggested that I should end meditation sessions with concentration on the head and with a smile. I used the technique of concentrating on the head regularly during the last stages and found it extremely beneficial for clearance of large chunks of denseness and, significantly so, effortlessly. I could, however, never muster a smile. Smiles in the last stages had become rare, reserved for times when I was not conscious of vibrations.

I met Sraddhalu again at the end of October 2002. I mentioned to him that I was still struggling to complete the preliminary stage. He suggested that I should devote some time every day to meditate on a spot around 1 centimetre above the crown that, according to Hindu belief, is the spot from where Divine light enters the body. I should then visualise pouring in of white light from that spot to fill the entire body, simultaneously expanding the body on all sides. I should then visualise that the fully expanded body is enveloped in a vast cover of white light. After a while, I should slowly move my concentration lower and lower, step by step, down to the eyes, with a pause at all the spots where the movement of concentration came across resistance.

I tried the technique but could not successfully concentrate from spot to spot in any order because of very heavy resistance from large chunks of denseness and damaged nerves. I would feel an utter chaos as if the nerves were going helter-skelter, with a very a mild pain. I found, however, that mere concentration on the spot above the crown produced very productive results in clearance of denseness and rectification of deflected nerves. I mentioned this to Sraddhalu who then asked me to abandon the second step.

Sraddhalu introduced me Ran Hicks who looked after the Aurobindo Ashram in Florida and suggested that I meet him. According to Ran Hicks, my consciousness was experiencing a strong gravitational pull. In other words, the ego was not letting the consciousness go. He also suggested the same technique as suggested by Sraddhalu of perceiving white light entering the body. Ran Hicks suggested two other measures – one, that I do Surya Namaskar as a part of yoga asanas and two, that I walk slowly for half an hour every day on the terrace and remain conscious of the surrounding vastness during the walk.

I started to experience flows of soft sensations during the last and final stage – a pleasant relief in the excruciatingly difficult stage. Soft or subtle sensations would flow for a very short while, followed by intense, powerful vibrations to work on rectification of deflected nerves with the usual attendant disquiet and discomfort. I had experienced soft vibrations only in the early stages; they disappeared after that, to reappear for short durations at the fag end, when some of the damaged nerves had been restored to normalcy. Would it be that I began to experience soft vibrations again in the last stages because the upper levels had already been cleared up?

The Physical and the Bio-Spiritual would undergo a havoc, clearance of large doses of denseness and considerable disturbance of the deflected nerves during meditation sessions in the last and final stages. The activity would not end there and then; the session would be followed by readjustment of the nerves. I acquired a definite impression that the subtle feelings in the upper parts of the body were due to the movement or readjustment of the deflected nerves in the lower levels. Could it be that when I (or for that matter anyone else) experienced subtle sensations in the initial stages, these sensations were due to some activity affecting the nervous system in the Bio-Spiritual? Obviously, I could not, at that stage, be conscious of it.

A thought kept on coming up again and again – is every soft vibration a subtle vibration, the difference between 'soft' and 'subtle' in my dictionary being that subtle vibrations bring about some spiritual change whereas soft vibrations were merely physically-likeable vibrations.

The entire process of clearance of denseness and healing of the inner nervous system was a prolonged, painful, tumultuous experience, resulting in a dramatic change in my sense of values and way of life. Besides other developments, I acquired a growing sense of detachment from all things external. I think that when you get so deeply involved, day and night, in the inner struggle, it is but natural that the outer matters would become inconsequential and insignificant.

The prolonged period of clearance of denseness and repairs to the nervous system necessarily involved intense pressure on almost each and every part of the body, including the seven spots where the chakras, the main centres or plexuses of sensory and motor nerves, are located in the body. The seven spots, as identified by both the Western and Indian spiritual philosophers, are the base of the spine (Muladhara chakra), over the spleen (Svathisthana chakra), the navel (Manipura chakra), over the heart (Anahata chakra), the throat (Visuddha chakra), the brow (Ajna chakra) and the crown (Sahasrara chakra). I think all the seven chakras began to awaken after January 2002.

On three or four occasions, I experienced consistent, prolonged pressure on six of the chakra spots, except the crown. In early January 2002, I experienced, for the first time, a strong pressure on the heart-centre, the point I used to meditate on. The pressure moved up to the throat, then the centre of the brow, then to the navel, over the spleen and lastly the lower end of the spine. It then moved back to the brow, the throat and then the heart-centre, removing denseness in the areas surrounding each chakra spot that may be called its own and the neighbouring territory.

A few days later, at the end of a long roving meditation session, there was pressure on each chakra in the back, from down, upward. The pressure was so intense as to violently shake up the body, with each chakra heavily heaving up and down. The head in particular was lifted up frequently and each time for a longer duration. The same operation occurred later in the front, starting from head, down to the navel. It stopped there, without moving lower. Whether the Force deliberately left out the lower two chakras or that it was tired, as it normally was after about 90 minutes work, I do not know. The Force had its own schedule; after about 90 minutes it used to stop, to resume its activity after a gap or rest of half an hour or so.

This was an unusual, strange experience. It felt as if the operation was intended to shake out some evil force that was in the body. It felt so, but cannot be because I do not believe in evil spirits. I believe that all untoward happenings are to a large extent an outcome of one's own doings, barring accidents. One may call them as evil spirits from the outside, to put blame on external agencies rather than owning responsibility for one's own misdeeds.

On another occasion, a flow started from the Muladhara chakra, a continuous flow till the whole body was filled with it. I think the flow from the lower part of the body is of two types — denseness and energy. The latter invariably moved towards the head, seeking, so to say, to meet with the crown, the Sahasrara chakra. Ancient Hindu spiritual philosophy says that the Sahasrara is the mate of Muladhara. As the head still had substantial denseness, the energy from the Muladhara could not meet the Sahasrara. It positioned itself, as it looked, way above the head. I thought that the work was over. It was, however, not so; the energy started clearing the obstructing parts below the head even after the session was terminated.

I had a remarkable experience early July in 2002. I woke up at around 2 a.m. with a congested throat and chest.

This was a signal to meditate and clear the denseness. I mediated in the shavasan position. After a little while, I felt as if I was in mid-air. This was an unusual feeling, which I had experienced only once earlier. A little while later, I noticed a peculiar sensation in the centre of my abdomen. The sensation kept on increasing. I then felt that I was floating in the air. Both the times, it was a gentle, pleasant sensation. I continued to meditate and felt a pressure in the centre of the brow. After some time, I saw a blue circle in the midst of a hazy, wider circle. Then the blue spot disappeared. After a little while, the blue spot reappeared, this time in a wider and clearer, whiter circle. The blue was sky blue in colour and the white was a radiant white. I thought that the navel or the Muladhara and the brow or Ajna chakras were being activated again.

I have to find out the significance of the floating feeling and of different coloured spots. And when do they appear? And why, and why so infrequently and why the long gap?

After reading Gopi Krishna's *Higher Consciousness*, it would seem that the upward shafts rising from the Muladhara region, termed as the Force II in the previous chapter, were the reproductive or vital energy. This is borne out by the fact that the denseness in from this region was thick and viscous, similar in texture to semen.

In the last and final stage, I experienced incessant flows of short waves of vital energy – wave after wave in rapid succession – rise above from the lower regions and it would race up like a tornado that cleared up chunks of denseness, the hooks and entanglement in a matter of seconds that would otherwise have otherwise involved long, laborious efforts. It seemed that the energy was in a hurry to finish off the job. Was this phenomenon another sign of the awakening of Kundalini?

According to Gopi Krishna, reproductive energy heals the injured nerves. Does it mean that the straightening out

The Journey Continues

of the deflected nerves was the handiwork of reproductive energy and not of Kundalini?

The most unusual experience occurred in early November 2002. I felt a flow of energy from the throat-centre, the Visuddha chakra, and covered the chest. After a few minutes, the flow stopped, followed by a sense of deep, indescribable sense of heavenly quietness. A little while later, the flow started again and this time it covered the abdomen. It stopped again, followed by the same peaceful quietness. The same phenomenon repeated itself twice more and by that time the Visuddha energy had covered the entire body below the throat.

After a lapse of some time, I experienced a flow of energy from the brow, not from the space between the eyebrows – the Ajna chakra – but from a point slightly above it. The energy filled the entire face. After it stopped, there was the same sense of peaceful, heavenly quietness.

A little later, the energy began to flow from the Sahasrara chakra and covered the entire head. This was the briefest of all the flows. The flow once again was followed by quietness.

Gopi Krishna says that with the awakening of Kundalini, one gets a cool feeling below the tongue and behind the palate. I started getting this feeling at the end of July 2002. In the course of time, the coolness spread to the eyes, and the brow, then the upper chest, the whole mouth and lasty the nose. In fact, until I read Gopi Krishna, I thought that the sense of coolness was a result of clearance of denseness in particular areas. That may, in fact, well be the case as Gopi Krishna's statement is unsupported by evidence.

Andrew Newberg and Eugene d'Aquili in *Why God Won't Go Away* say that the human nervous system has developed over centuries from the Neolithic times. The main developments comprise longer nerve loops and new dangling nerves. Does it mean in that it would not be incorrect to conjecture that in spiritually developed people or those who begin to develop spiritually, the nervous system undergoes further distinctive changes such as highly flexible or supple and super-sensitive nerves?

In the very last stages, I had a feeling that the body had lost some of its grossness. I could feel pockets of denseness in the ordinary course of life, slight heaviness and dull pain in some of the parts where large quantity of denseness yet remained. I got a definite impression that the Physical and Bio-Spiritual were getting merged.

Many a time I felt that an outside object or a person that I had seen a few seconds ago, was within my body. Was it that the body consciousness was becoming larger, more expanded, encompassing outside objects? Time will tell!

***

My cultivated code of conduct got crystallised during the long time involved on the first stage. Besides growing detachment from material matters, the other noteworthy features were the growing absence of feeling of fear or sense of insecurity, growing absence of depression and even sense of disappointment, much less anger and habit of criticising of others. They say that spiritual growth leads to enlargement of love – love for living beings at large. I certainly developed a greater sense of consideration for others but did not see any evidence of love for all.

What happened to me or with me, I believe, is nothing extraordinary or unique. As Sri Aurobindo says, the Tapas or the force of consciousness brings about the change, slowly and gradually (*Synthesis of Yoga*).

In a sense, there is, therefore, nothing spiritually unique about anyone. The machinery for transformation is provided by Nature in everyone. Mechanics of change may differ from person to person and, in that sense, one can say that that each person is unique. However, the principle of change as also its direction is a common, a universal

The Journey Continues

phenomenon. What are needed to put the machinery to work are will and faith. I think that the will – the will to pursue the path without wilting – is the starting and all-important point. One does not have to have faith in the perfection of the machinery or in the force of consciousness in the beginning, as it was in my case. However, the faith does get developed on its own, automatically.

According to Sri Aurobindo, even the stages of change or spiritual development are already set within the self as three in number – 'the attempt of the ego to enter into contact' with the Divine, 'laborious preparation of the lower nature' and 'eventual transformation'. As per Sri Aurobindo, the last stage is the fastest, but it is a long, long way to go to experience its truth.

I started the journey as a rationalist. I believed that whatever I could not see or whatever could not be rationally explained, did not exist and was a product of imagination or fantasy. The change that has taken place is dramatic. I no longer look for reason alone and believe in understanding and mostly understanding with something that is beyond reason.

In the last stages, I mostly concentrated on a spot a little above the heart-centre. I observed six nerves emanating from the spot. It was not just a dot, but a sort of a rectangle. The six nerves were – the first one was parallel to the spine and extending beyond the spine at both ends; the second nerve extended sideways to the left and right across the chest; the third and the fourth nerves ran across from the left and the right shoulder crossways to the side ends of the pelvis; the fifth and the sixth were also crossway nerves at just a little distance from the ends of the third and the fourth, between the pelvis and the collar nerves. The six nerves together formed twelve spokes fanning out from the heart-centre – six going upward and six downward – remarkably the number equal to the number of spokes that are said to emanate from Anahata chakra.

The Reality

How have other authors interpreted the various concepts? Here are some of them:

1. **Indian Caste System**

    Georges Van Vrekhem, in his book *The Mother*, points out that there was caste system even in Europe in the 19th century. The system comprised four classes as in India – the clergy (Brahmin), the nobility (kshatrya), the merchants (vaishya) and the common worker (shudra). The European caste system had its roots in the Middle Ages. 'Thanks to the philosophical evolution of the European mind during the Renaissance, the Enlightenment and the French Revolution, the dominant classes of the clergy and the nobility (had) lost most of their privileges and the bourgeois class (had taken) took over.'

    India still struggles under the yoke of a caste system, though much of the old system has withered away.

2. **Evolution**

    This is a generally accepted as a scientific fact. In India it has existed for centuries as a spiritual fact (Georges Van Vrekhem, *The Mother*).

The Reality

3. **Consciousness:**

   3.1   There are two main characteristics of ordinary consciousness.

   One is ego, a self that exists as a distinct reality, separate from the rest of the universe. We are so firmly tied up to the ego that it is difficult to conceive of life without it. In this context, Carl Jung says, 'If there is no ego, there is nobody to be conscious of anything.' The ego is 'therefore indispensable to the conscious process'. Yet, meditation leads to a complete transformation of consciousness and in Mother's words 'a reversal of consciousness'.

   The second characteristic is what Sri Aurobindo calls 'psychological ignorance'. We are so immersed in ordinary consciousness, that we lose sight of the unconscious self which, in fact, constitutes nine-tenths of the total psyche.

   3.2   The cultivated code of conduct I mentioned in 'The Force: Stage One' was a mere readjustment, and not a real change.

   3.3   'Our observable consciousness, that which we call ourselves, is only the little visible part of our being. It is a small field below which are depths and further depths and widths and ever wider widths which support and supply it but to which it has no visible access. All that is our self, our being – what we see at the top is only our ego and its visible nature.' (Sri Aurobindo, *Essays Divine and Human*).

   3.4   Sri Aurobindo says that there are two ways of looking at the formation of consciousness (Soumitra Basu, 'Integral Psychotherapy – Personal Encounters').

Outer being comprising physical, vital and mental, and revolving around the ego.

Inner being with a midway level of consciousness comprising inner physical, inner mental and inner vital. The inner being possesses intuition, can get inklings of the future, strengthens will, can make actions supple and subtle, sensitises the physical to have visions, hear inner voices and feel auras. It is the meeting ground of the individual and universal consciousness.

3.5 In the paper 'Sri Aurobindo's Metaphysical Psychology' presented in the Second International Conference on Integral Psychology, Puducherry, Arabinda Basu lists the following salient points of Sri Aurobindo's understanding of consciousness:

One: 'Consciousness is not a phenomenon; it does not depend on the reactions of the personality to stimulus from outside or on mental activities. When the mind falls silent and ceases to function, consciousness abides.'

Two: 'Consciousness is immobile. Consciousness is not only a power of knowledge of self and things, it is or has dynamic and creative energy. It is free to act or not to act and free in action and inaction.'

Three: 'It is Universal.'

Four: 'Consciousness is the self . . . the cosmic soul.'

Five: 'Consciousness is self-luminous. . . . It is not revealed by anything other than itself; indeed, it is in the light of consciousness that everything is revealed and known.'

4. The Psychic Being

It is 'the true evolving in my nature.' (Sri Aurobindo, *The Synthesis of Yoga*). Georges Van Vrekhem says, 'For this reason, the realisation of the psychic being was considered by Sri Aurobindo and the Mother as the first and fundamental of the three essential realisations of their yoga, the other two being the spiritual and supramental.'

5. Thoughts

5.1 'Our minds are like a market place,' said the Mother. 'We don't realise it, but we could hardly call one thought out of a hundred our own, bathing as we do in the whirling sea of thoughts all around us.' (Georges Van Vrekhem, *The Mother*).

5.2 According to C.W. Leadbeater in *The Chakras*, 'Masses of thoughts are very definite things, occupying a place in space. Thoughts on the same subject and of the same character tend to aggregate; therefore for many subjects there is a thought centre, a definite space in the atmosphere and other thoughts about the same matter are attracted to such a centre, and go to increase its size and influence. A thinker may in this way contribute to a centre, but he in turn may be influenced by it; and this is one of the reasons why people think in droves, like sheep.'

6. Human's Physical Development

From the origin as a primate, it has taken about four million years, according to recent estimates (Georges Van Vrekhem).

7. Four Hindu Goddesses

Maheshwari: Goddess of supreme knowledge; Mahakal: Goddess of supreme strength; Mahalakshmi:

Goddess of the supreme love and delight; and Mahasarawati: Goddess of divine skills and of the works of the spirit.

8. **Human Form**

   According to the Indian tradition, it is only after millions of births (eight million, four hundred thousand, to be exact) that the ascending soul takes the form of a human being (Gopi Krishna, *Higher Consciousness*).

9. **Will**

   'Will is expressed in the face; its result is implanted in the countenance.' (J.T. Kent, *Homoeopathic Philosophy*).

10. **Miracles**

    According to Eckhart Tolle in *The Power of Now*, when you become conscious of your inner self or inner consciousness, you become aware of your Being, which is a part the Universal Being. You can then 'perceive another person's body and mind as just a screen, as it were, behind which you can feel their true reality, as you feel yours. So, when confronted with someone else's suffering or unconscious behaviour, you stay present and in touch with Being and are thus able to look beyond the form and feel the other person's radiant and pure Being through your own. . . . Miracles of healing sometime occur through this realisation, by awakening Being-consciousness in others – if they are ready.'

11. **New Age**

    All spiritual philosophers talk of the New Age when everyone and everything will become enlightened and so does Eckhart Tolle. He quotes the New Testament Book of Revelation, 'Then I saw a new heaven and a new earth, for the first heaven and the first earth had passed away.'

12. God

The word God has become empty of meaning through thousands of years of misuse.' (Eckhart Tolle, *The Power of Now*).

12.1 'The word God is limiting ... because it implies an entity other than you. God is Being itself, not a being. There can be no subject–object relationship here, no duality, no you and God.' (Eckhart Tolle, *The Power of Now*).

12.2 According to ancient Indian philosophy, belief in God was not a restricted view. It covered 'an anthropomorphic God or a multitude of gods, or a God without form, or a Transcendent Reality (Gopi Krishna, *Kundalini: The Secret of Yoga*).

13. Addictions

13.1 One looks for an escape from mind-activity by getting to a level of consciousness that is below thought. This happens during sleep but also 'to some extent though sex, alcohol and other drugs that suppress excessive mind activity'. But for these addictions, 'the insanity of the human mind would become even more glaringly obvious than it is already.'

13.2 There is a deeper cause for addictions. Tolle says, 'Every addiction arises from an unconscious refusal and move through your own pain. Every addiction starts with pain and ends with pain. . . . That is why after the initial euphoria has passed, there is so much unhappiness, so much pain in intimate relationships.'

13.3 Similarly, Tolle says, people dream of future to escape pain that the present holds. 'The first thing that they might encounter if they focused their attention on the Now is their own pain.' (Tolle, *The Power of Now*).

14. **Arguments**

    'An argument implies identification, as well as resistance and reaction to other person's position. The result is that the polar opposites become mutually energised. These are the mechanics of unconsciousness. You can still make your point clearly and firmly, but there will be no reactive force behind it, no defence or attack.' (Tolle, *The Power of Now*).

15. **Psychological Time**

    15.1 The expression has been coined by Tolle to signify 'identification with the past and continuous compulsive projection in top the future'. In this context he asks, 'Are your thought processes creating guilt, pride, resentment, anger, regret or self-pity? Then you are not only reinforcing a false sense of self but also helping to accelerate your body aging process by creating an accumulation of past on your psyche.' (Tolle, *The Power of Now*).

    15.2 'Time is not a continuum. It is an element of relativity that exists vertically, not horizontally.... Don't think of it as "left to right" thing. . . . Time is an "up and down" thing! It is a spindle, representing the eternal moment of Now.' (Neale Donald Walsch, *Conversations with God*, Book 2)

    15.3 'It is you who are moving, not time. Time has no movement. There is only One Moment.' (Neale Donald Walsch, *Conversations with God*, Book 2).

16. **Cycles: Nature's Law**

    16.1 'Growth is usually considered positive but nothing can grow for ever. If growth, of whatever kind, were to go on and on, it would eventually become monstrous and destructive. Dissolution is needed for new growth to happen. One cannot exist without the other.' (Tolle, *The Power of Now*).

The Reality

16.2 'A cycle can last for anything from a few hours to a few years.'

16.3 'The cyclical nature of the universe is closely linked with the impermanence of all things and situations. The Buddha made this a central part of his teaching.'

16.4 Jesus said, 'Do not lay up for yourselves treasures on earth, where moth and rust consume and where thieves break in and steal.' (Tolle, *The Power of Now*).

16.5 'I think we are all God-and that we are constantly, every one of us, journeying from Knowing to Not Knowing again, from being to not being again, from Oneness to Separation to Oneness again, in a never-ending cycle. That is the cycle of life – what you call the Cosmic Wheel.' (Donald Neale Walsch, *Conversations with God*, Book 3)

17. Myths

17.1 The Neanderthals viz. in the Stone Age, some 20 lakh years ago, buried their dead with some ceremonies and with clothes, tools, weapons and other essentials obviously in the belief that there was life after death The paraphernalia buried along with the dead was to equip the departed with essentials for the next life.

17.2 Two important conclusions flow:

   a. Neanderthals were conscious of inevitability of death

   b. 'They had already found a way to defeat or cope with it, at least conceptually.' (A. Newberg and E. d'Aquili, *Why God Won't Go Away*).

17.3 It is also obvious that from very early times itself humans thought about the deepest mysteries of life. Myths owe their origin to the enigmas of life and death, and were created as a device to put the mind at rest about them.

17.4 Myths continue to remain; people all over and everywhere believe in them – in myths about Jesus, Lord Rama and Krishna, the Buddha and others.

17.5 Newberg and d'Aquili say that contrary to modern usage, myth is not 'fable' or 'fantasy'. The origin of myth is Greek 'mythos' that translates 'word' but spoken with 'deep, unquestioned authority.'

17.6 Quoting a renowned scholar Joseph Campbell, the two writers say, 'Myths show us how to be human. They show us what is most important and what, in terms of the inner life, is most deeply and profoundly true. . . . The lasting myths of past cultures all contain psychological and spiritual truths that resonate with psyche and spirits of readers today.'

17.7 They add, 'Essentially all myths can be reduced to a simple framework. First, they focus upon a crucial existential concern – the creation of the world, for example, or how evil came to be. Next, they frame that concern as a pair of apparently irreconcilable opposites – heroes and monsters, gods and humans, life and death, heaven and hell. Finally, and most important, myths reconcile those opposites through the action of gods or other spiritual posers in a way that relieves us of our existential concerns.'

17.8 The authors ask a crucial question, 'Why are the myths of all world culture so strikingly, consistently similar?'

The Reality

17.9 According to them, 'Cultural disposition can account for some of those similarities – myths were often borrowed from culture to culture and then shaped to fit the local needs.' However, 'what gives them such universal power that the same essential stories would be as appealing to people in environments as different as those inhabited by Inuits, Hebrews, Incas and Celts.'

17.10 Based on some views expressed by Carl Jung and Joseph Campbell and their own research, the authors conclude that, 'Myths are created by basic, universal aspects of the brain, in particular, the fundamental neurological processes through which the brain makes sense of the world. Although culture and psychology may influence them significantly, it's the neurological grounding of mythic stories that gives them their staying power, as well as the authority with which they resolve our existential fears.'

18. Rituals

18.1 The major goal of rituals is to transcend the self and possibly to merge the self into a larger reality. Rituals are usually performed in groups – small or big. Group rituals, in early times, 'performed an important survival function by fostering among, a given clan or tribe, a sense of specialness and common destiny.' (A. Newberg and E. d'Aquili, *Why God Won't Go Away*).

18.2 The two authors point out that research conducted by a few scientists has led to the view that rituals may have biological roots. 'Studies have shown that participating in certain spiritual behaviours such as prayer, religious services, meditation, and physical exertion can lower blood pressure, decrease heart rate, lower rates of respiration, reduce levels of the hormone cortisol, and create positive changes in immune system function.'

18.3 As per Newberg and d'Aquili, ritual process, meditation, chanting, contemplative prayer and the like activities affect the body's quiescent and arousal systems. When the rhythmic behaviour in rituals becomes fast 'the arousal system is driven to higher and higher levels of activation'. When the activation reaches excessively high level, one part of the brain (hippocampus) slows down the neural flows to another part of the brain (orientation association area, OAA) that 'helps us distinguish the self from the rest of the world and orients the self in the sense of space'. As a result, the second part of the brain, OAA, 'which requires constant neutral flows' is rendered ineffective leading to 'a softer, less precise definition of the boundaries of self or to a unitary experience or the merger of the individual self with the universal self'.

18.4 Scientific studies have 'demonstrated that that rhythmic behaviour (in rituals, slow bending or bowing in prayers, prostration, etc.) simultaneously activates several senses at once'.

18.5 The authors also say that the ritual actions may result in activation of a part of the brain called amygdala that would lead to 'arousal response... (which) blended with blissful calm of the hyper quiescent state... might be experienced as "religious awe"'. The feeling of awe might also get intensified by 'a benedictive bow during a prayer' or a sense of smell of incense and other fragrances used in religious rites.

19. Mysticism

19.1 Modern day rationalistic thinking treats experiences like a visit by Jesus or Lord Krishna as a result of psychological imbalance. Medical science calls them a delusion. Psychiatrists believe that 'Mystical experiences are illusions triggered by the neurotic, regressive urge to reject an unfulfilling reality, and recapture the bliss we knew as infants, bathed in the safe and all-encompassing unity of mother's love. . . . In modern usage, "mysticism", like its linguistic cousin "myth", is often used pejoratively to dismiss sloppy or superstitious thinking.'

19.2 Gopi Krishna, in *Kundalini: The Secret of Yoga* calls mystical experiences such as vision of God, goddesses or a revered religious personality as hallucinatory, or a result of self-hypnosis. He says that in a state of 'super-sensory form of awareness, in contact now with the subtle universe of consciousness that was previously impervious to (his) inner vision . . . the idea already existing or inculcated about the Deity or the Superconscious state acting as a suggestion . . . can create a hallucinatory appearance corresponding to it which has all the semblance of reality.'

19.3 Andrew Newberg and E. d'Aquili quote the research conducted Jeffery Saver and John Robin who outlined the significant elements of mystic experiences: (a) strong contradictory emotions – fear with joy, (b) non-existence of sense of time and space, (c) intuitive way of understanding in place rational thinking, (d) intimations of the presence of the sacred or the holy, and (e) a rapturous stale that has been described as 'in interior illumination of reality that results in ultimate freedom.'

19.4 Despite different techniques deployed by mystics in different climes and cultures – Sufis, Christianity, Taoism, Zen, Kabbalistic Jews, Hindus and others – it is remarkable that there is strong similarity 'in mystic experience of being one with God and God in man.' The descriptions emerged independently.

In respect of the rationalist view that mystic experiences are the outcome of a deluded mind, the authors say that 'science, however, has not been to empirically prove that mysticism is a product of distraught or dysfunctional minds Significant research, in fact, seems to show that people who experience genuine mystical states enjoy much higher levels of psychological health than public at large.'

At the same time, 'there is evidence to support that . . . certain pathological conditions such as schizophrenia and temporal lobe epilepsy can trigger voices, visions, and other hallucinatory effect that often possess religious connotations, and that occasionally these hallucinations can lead to an abnormal fascination with spiritual affairs.' However, the distinction between the mystics and psychotics lies clearly and distinctly between these responses to similar experiences:

a. **Vision, voices, events:** Psychotics get confused and frightened because their experiences are distressing in nature as normally it is an angry reproachful God that they see. Mystics, however, experience ecstatic joy, a spiritual unity in terms of wholeness and serenity and love.

The Reality

    b. **Break with normal reality:** Psychotics experience compulsive withdrawal and are deeply pushed into social isolation. In their case, the delusional state may last for years. Mystics, on the other hand, welcome the feeling of withdrawal; they function effectively in society and they share their experiences with others with clarity.

    c. **Meaning of experiences:** Psychotics interpret their experiences in terms of religious grandiosity; they acquire an inflated ego and imagine themselves as special emissaries of God, with special healing powers. Spiritualists, on the other hand, experience a loss of pride and ego, quieting of the mind and emptying of the self.

    (A. Newberg and E. d'Aquili, *Why God Won't Go Away*)

19.5 Besides psychotics, pathological conditions or epileptic seizures result in similar experiences as spirituality such as sudden ecstasy, religious awe, increased interest in religion, even religious conversions, out-of-body experiences and perceived presence of God. However, mystic experiences are more convincing.

19.6 However, once again, there are distinct qualitative differences between the two types of experiences:

    a. **Seizures:** In pathological cases, seizures strike regularly till the cause is removed. In spiritualism, seizures are few and far between in an entire lifetime.

    b. **Hallucinations:** In pathological cases, hallucinations are consistent and repetitive in pattern – hearing the same voice with the same message. Moreover, hallucinations involve a single sensory system – see a vision, hear a disembodied voice or feel a presence. Spiritual experiences are variable; one gets different messages. Moreover, the experiences are multi-sensory; they simply feel real.

In pathological cases, hallucination also feel real but afterwards, on return to normal consciousness, they become fragmented and dreamlike and appear as mistakes of the mind. In spiritual experiences, one can never be persuaded that the experiences were not real and the sense of realness never fades away or dissipate over time.

(A. Newberg and E. d'Aquili, *Why God Won't Go Away*).

19.7 Notwithstanding all this, many researchers have found compelling similarity between epilepsy and spirituality and have posthumously diagnosed history's greatest mystics as suffering from epilepsy, for example, Mohammed who saw visions and heard voices, Joan of Arc who saw lights, Saint Teresa of Avila who saw visions, Vincent Van Gogh because of hyper-religiosity.

19.8 Authors point out that mystical or unitary experiences happen to all of us, all the time. 'Humans, in fact, are natural mystics blessed with an inborn genius for effortless self-transcendence.' One loses oneself in a beautiful piece of music, or gets swept away by a patriotic speech. However, there is an essential difference in the degree of experience between 'ordinary' and 'profound' mystical experiences.

19.9 'Although . . . emerging field of neurotheology (refers to Andrew Newberg's research) is certainly fascinating, and does demonstrate clearly that the brains of healthy mystics are

The Reality

not like those of schizophrenics, it does not answer the conundrum of whether the spiritual experience is an illusion created by the brain, or the brain's perception of an actual reality. James (a scientist of 19th century) 'suggested that we take a phenomenological and pragmatic stance towards spiritual experience, that is, that we explore its subjective qualities and judge these by their fruits of life.' (Michael Miovic, 'Towards a Spiritual Philosophy').

19.10 'Just because the human mind may never know whether or not God exists in an absolutely final sense, does not alter the fact that, in the end, it either does or not. Atoms existed long before humans knew them to be pervasive, and likewise God, if in fact does exist, does so independently of our current judgments – and is equally pervasive as atoms.' (Michael Miovic, 'Towards a Spiritual Philosophy').

19.11 In his book *The Initiation*, Donald Schnell, a German, who was an avid bodybuilder, recounts his experiences of how he got initiated as a swami by Swami Nagananda and met Babaji. He says, 'Babaji works through the prophets in every era to guide human evolution. His purpose is to inspire you to remove the conditions of war, and racial and religious prejudices. . . . Babaji was last seen in the 1800s when he gave spiritual initiation to Sri Lahiri Mhasaya, a famous yogi saint. He appeared to Mahasaya's student Yukteshwar and to Yukteshwar's student Paramahansa Yogananda. Babaji's body continuously regenerates itself and, therefore, it 'shows no signs of age. He continues to appear to be in early twenties, even though he has lived may be thousand years.'

Schnell says that from early childhood, from the age of seven, he was interested in spiritualism, keen to understand his connection with God and to meet spiritual masters. From the age of eight, he got attracted to Babaji and used to be fascinated by the drawing of Babaji in the Paramahansa Yogananada's famous book *Autobiography of a Yogi*. He met Babaji eventually 34 years later, in 1997, in India before he was initiated as a swami by his guru, Swami Nagananda.

Schnell describes in detail his 3-4 meetings with Babaji. During some of these meetings, he felt the presence and interacted with Swami Yogananda who was in fact in a distant place at that time. He also met Swami Yogananda who was no longer alive. Schnell's accounts clearly indicate that he went into trance three or four times. It seems that he saw these persons while he was in trance. Both Nagananda and Yogananda occupied a prominent presence in Schnell's subconscious and emerged as real persons in the trance.

20. Yoga

20.1 'The word yoga derives from the root 'yug' (to yoke), and connotation of 'yoking' the human back to the Divine is similar to 'religion' which derives from Latin 'religere' (to the back). (Michael Miovic, 'Towards a Spiritual Psychology: Bridging Psychodynamic Psychotherapy with Integral Yoga'.)

20.2 According to ancient Hindu philosophy, when religion was all-pervading, as a way of life, as against the modern attitude that religion is purely a personal matter, yoga was, as stated by Gopi Krishna, 'an adjunct to religion' and meant to

The Reality

'to prove . . . the validity of religious doctrines.' (*Kundalini: The Secret of Yoga*).

21. **Faith**

    Faith in a higher power who would guide and protect humans through all the vicissitudes of life has tremendous physical and mental benefits. In a more exalted sense, faith 'becomes an impersonal refuge of ultimate spiritual wholeness and truth, in which believers can find transcendent release from the sufferings of life. . . . (It) may also have been a crucial reason human race has managed to survive.' (A. Newberg and E. d'Aquili, *Why God Won't Go Away*).

22. **Fear**

    'Fear is responsible for dissociation, rigidity, defensive ego and compensatory desires. Freedom from fear leads to flexibility, spontaneity and unitiveness which is the same as self-control or will.' (V. George Matthew, 'Models of Consciousness and Its Transformation').

23. **Well-Being**

    Talking of differences between the West and the East in respect of concept of well-being, K. Krishna Mohan, in has paper 'Spirituality and Well Being: An Overview' says 'that the conceptualisations made in the West revolve around the ability to satisfy one's needs. . . . In the Indian tradition, control over the senses is thought to be essential to well-being. . . . While in the West the idea is to have control or exploit the environment since it is thought that the environment provides the inputs that lead to need satisfaction, in Hindu spiritual thought the concept of "being in tune" with the environment is encouraged to be able to experience well-being.'

24. Listening

24.1 Vimala Thakkar in *Personal Discovery of Truth* relates the incident about J. Krishnamurthy who was in the habit of asking the people gathered to listen to him as to what they were listening. Krishnamurthy explained that listening required 'the innocency of the attitude of learning'. He said that people would come to evaluate him, 'to compare what I say with what they have known. This is not listening'.

24.2 Elsewhere, Vimala Thakkar describes listening as 'as creative a movement as speaking is'.

25. Enlightenment

Vimla Thakkar (*Personal Discovery of Truth*) calls liberation and enlightenment as 'freedom from the known . . . Freedom the impurity of imbalances . . . an invisible peace and silence within – that is an indication of Enlightenment'.

26. Reincarnation

According to David Schnell (*The Initiation*), 'About four-fifths of the world's population believes in reincarnation. Reincarnation was even an accepted fact of Christianity, until it was excised from the Bible by church fathers in the fifth century.'

27. Prayer

27.1 'Prayer and meditation are the two wings of the bird. . . . The bird cannot fly with only one wing. Prayer is certainly meditation. It is a spoken form of meditation, an active form, delivered with love.' (David Schnell, *The Initiation*).

27.2 Prayer is surrender, an ego-less plea for help, delivered with earnestness and faith or love. In that sense it is meditation. But meditation is more than prayer. Besides, surrender and faith, there is commitment and aspiration.

28. Magnetism

According to C.W.L. Leadbeater (*The Chakras*) a human body is composed of a gross part and a subtle or etheric part. Energy or vitality in the body is produced by food and air. Along with the food and air, we take in the etheric matter. The etheric matter is circulated along the nerves by a fluid that is the person's 'own nerve-fluid, specialised within the spine, and composed of the primary life-force intermingled with the kundalini. . . . Etheric matter is constantly being thrown off from the pores, just as is gaseous matter, so that when two persons are close together, each necessarily absorbs much of the physical emanations of the other.' These emanations are magnetic energy.

The Transformation

1. **The Urge**

    1.1 Most writers on Yoga or meditation prescribe a number of pre-requisites prior to the start of serious meditation. Gopi Krishna lists them as 'self-denial, control of the senses, detachment from the world, truth and right conduct'. (Gopi Krishna, *Kundalini: The Secret of Yoga*).

    1.2 All living beings – humans, animals, vegetation – naturally possess the urge and capability to grow physically. Proper environment and conscious effort or care would, of course, ensure faster, balanced growth. However, even if these aids or instruments are not available, every living organism still grows and occasionally some develop into sturdier and stronger or livelier beings than those that have been given or received care and attention.

    1.3 Humans are unique amongst living forms to be bestowed with the urge and capacity to grow spiritually. The spiritual seed is embedded in everyone and all of us are, consciously or unconsciously, undergoing spiritual evolution.

The Transformation

When the 'unconscious' ones become conscious of the hidden urge due to one or more reasons and begin to seriously look within and make a firm resolve to bring about a change in life style, the inner self automatically then begins to change. It is a remarkable fact that one necessarily develops a sense of detachment and control of the senses and adopts right and true conduct, true to one's personality – three of the list of four necessary ingredients for spiritual path listed by Gopi Krishna.

1.4 In other words, whilst it would be certainly helpful to possess the qualities listed as prerequisites, it is by no means essential to have them to be able to seriously venture on the spiritual path. What is essential is a strong, conscious urge to change and remain steadfast in the desire to objectively look within, undeterred by the painful revelations about one's true personality.

1.5 In fact, after one enters the field of consciousness, the self, as Sri Aurobindo says, begins 'to turn towards the Divine Truth as the sunflower towards the sun . . . and draws back from all that is perversion or denial of it, from all that is false and undivine.' (*The Synthesis of Yoga*).

1.6 Self-denial is the fifth ingredient in the list given by Gopi Krishna. He holds the view that this is an extreme injunction. In this context he says, 'One of the greatest of . . . sages, Yajnavalkya, discredits severe austerity and self-mortification as effective means for Brahman realisation. In the *Mandaka Upanishad*, continence, truth and performance of prescribed duties are considered to be sufficient measures for the attainment of higher consciousness. The Bhagavad Gita strongly condemns excessive penance and self-mortification, preaching moderation, selfless action, devotion, truth and righteousness as the most appropriate virtues of those who seek enlightenment.'

2. **The Turning Point**

    2.1 'The edge is where new opportunity lies. The edge is where true creation begins.' (Neale Donald Walsch, *Conversations with God*, Book 2).

    2.2 'Come to the edge,' he said.

    'We can't We are afraid,' they responded.

    'Come to the edge,' he said.

    'We can't. We will fall,' they responded.

    'Come to the edge,' he said.

    And they came.

    And he pushed them

    And they flew.

    (The French poet-philosopher Guillaume Apollinaire)

Body, Denseness, Nervous System, Chakras, Kundalini

1. **Integral Yoga**
   Aurobindo builds his concept of Integral Yoga on the essential basis of transformation of the body.

2. **The Body Cells**

    2.1 The Mother talks of changes in the body. Georges Van Vrekhem quotes the following from *The Mother: Prayers and Meditations* (words in brackets are mine):

The Transformation

'Thou hast taken entire possession of this miserable instrument and if it is not yet perfected enough for them to complete its transformation, Thou art at work in each (*of its cells to knead it and make it supple and* enlighten it and in the whole being to arrange, organise and enlighten it. Everything is in movement, everything is changing) . . .'

Elsewhere, she talks of 'all the pain, all that suffering, everything'.

2.2 The Mother talked of changes to the cells. She did not talk of nerves. However, nerves are, after all, a conglomeration of cells like every other part of the body and, therefore, when the body undergoes a change or transformation, the change would be effected through changed cells.

2.3 Elsewhere, the Mother talks of 'all the pain, all that suffering, everything' Whilst my body underwent changes during only the preliminary stage and the Mother's body changed for peak advanced purpose of divinisation of matter and the body, yet I found the nerves being 'kneaded'. I also found that the nerves had become supple for straightening out. I also experienced constant 'movement' in the body.

3. Sleeplessness

'It is true that for a long time I have not slept in the usual sense of the word. That is to say, at no time do I fall back into unconsciousness which is the sign of ordinary sleep. But I give my body the rest it needs, that is, two or three hours of lying down in an absolute immobility, but in which the whole being, mental, psychic, vital and physical, enters into a complete rest made of perfect peace, absolute silence and total immobility, while the consciousness remains completely awake.' (La Mere, *Glimpses of the Mother's Life*, Volume 2).,

4. **Impurities**

Sri Aurobindo, in a rare piece talks of impurities in the body in his poem 'A God's Labour':

I have been digging deep and long

Mid a horror of filth and mire

A bed for the golden river's song

A home for the deathless fire ...

(Sri Aurobindo, *Collected Poems*)

5. **Transformation of the Body**

5.1 The transformation of the body is a difficult task, 'The consciousness of each cell has to surrender . . . the cells carry within them the burden, hardened into a behavioural habit, of a catastrophic past.' (Georges Van Vrekhem, *The Mother*)

5.2 *It is an interesting thought. However, like most writers on spiritualism. Vrekhem does not substantiate his statement by any scientific evidence.*

5.3 During Stage One, I found nothing else except deflected nerves and as the nerves straightened out, the straight nerves also disappeared, replaced by, so to say, a void full only of vibrations. The following description of supramental body by the Mother in *Questions and Answers 1956* (Collected Works of the Mother, 8: 398) is similar to what I observed. I do not imply that my body reached the supramental stage – far from it – but maybe what I observed would be one aspect of the supramental body.

The Transformation

5.4 'Transformation implies that the whole purely material set-up (of the human body as it is now) be replaced by a set-up of concentration of force consisting of certain types of vibrations which replace each organ by a centre of conscious energy, moved by a conscious will and directed by a movement coming from above, from the higher regions. No stomach any longer, no heart, no circulation, no lungs, etc. . . . Naturally, no bones are needed in the system, for it is no longer a skeleton with skin and viscera, it is something different: it is concentrated energy obeying the will.'

5.5 I did not feel any 'conscious energy' nor 'concentrated energy'. I was too involved in observing the drama of how deflected nerves behaved or moved and what happened to them once they got straightened out.

6. Inner Body

6.1 My entry into the inner body was not a unique experience. Eckhart Tolle in *The Power of Now* devotes considerable attention to it.

6.2 'In your natural state of connectedness with the Being, this deeper reality can be felt every moment as the invisible inner body, the animating presence within you. So to "inhabit the body" is to feel tire body from within, to feel the life inside the body and thereby come to know that you are beyond the outer form.'

6.3 'The feeling of your inner body is formless, limitless, and unfathomable.'

6.4 'The inner body lies at the threshold between your form identity and your essence identity, your true nature. Never lose touch with it.'

6.5 'The Inner body is your link with the Unmanifested, and in its deepest aspect IS the Unmanifested – the Source from which consciousness emanates as the light emanates from the sun. Awareness of the inner body is consciousness remembering its origin and returning to the Source.'

6.6 Tolle describes the physical and psychological benefits of staying in touch with the inner body:

   a. Slowing down of the aging of the physical body
   b. Strengthening of the immune system
   c. A potent form of self-healing
   d. Strengthening of the psychic immune system that 'protects you from the negative mental-emotional force fields of others, which are highly contagious. Inhabiting the body protects not by putting up a shield, but raising the frequency of vibration of your total energy field, so that anything that vibrates at a lower frequency, such as fear, anger, depression, and so on, now exists in what is virtually a different order of reality. It does not enter your field of consciousness anymore, or if it does you don't need to offer any resistance to it because it passes right through you.'

6.7 'Meditation has been shown to alter the release of hormones . . . which help regulate blood pressure, thyroid-stimulating hormones and testosterone.' (A. Newberg and E. d'Aquili, *Why God Won't Go Away*).

7. The Nervous System

'The meticulous description of the nadis and the stress on their number provides further evidence that the ancient masters referred to the carriers of impulses and sensations in the body – in other words, to the nerves. The statement that there are thousands of nadis, fine like a spider's thread or hairy fiber of a lotus stalk, is a clear indication that they are the nerves made of flesh and not any imaginary astral conduits.' (Uri Geller, 'The Physical Aspects of Higher Consciousness')

8. **The Chakras**

   It is believed that there are seven chakras, all located at pivotal points in the body, mostly on the spinal cord. The spots command the organs of reproduction, elimination, digestion, blood circulation, respiration, ideation and the modalities of consciousness. As Gopi Krishna points put in *Higher Consciousness*, there is a natural and essential involvement 'of all the important organs of the body in the process of transformation'.

9. **Kundalini**

   9.1 It is 'the upward streaming of the reproductive energy' that shoots up to the brain through the cerebero-spinal axis. 'The upward flow . . . occurs spontaneously' and is a natural biological function. 'In fact, as is generally held, the sublimation of sexual energy usually occurs to an appreciable degree in the case of men of genius, great intellectuals, poets, painters, musicians and the like.' Gopi Krishna calls the sublimated sexual energy as the life-force. (Gopi Krishna, *Higher Consciousness*).

   9.2 'This physiological phenomenon has been known in India for at least four thousand years and is symbolically represented in every temple and shrine in which lingam or lingam and yoni, as creative symbols, are housed for adoration.'

9.3 The upward climb of the life-force 'without our awareness heals the injured cells and revitalises the weak areas in our brains to enable the evolutionary adjustments to proceed unimpeded'. Thus, according to Gopi Krishna, the evolutionary mechanism in the human body consists of the brain, the nervous system and the life-energy. However, kundalini is 'not uniformly effective in all men and women but varies enormously . . . depending on the vital organs and physical and mental traits of different individuals'. Other relevant factors are: sincerity and keenness of the seeker, 'heredity, noble traits of character, benevolent disposition'.

9.4 'In every case of a successful awakening, leading to a transformation of consciousness metabolic processes, the flow of reproductive secretions, and the circulation of transmuted energy, would be definitely noticed for varying lengths of time.'

9.5 Once the biological processes are started, they continue to work in a rhythmical fashion in the same way they function in the normal course. The uncertainty and unreliability is . . . entirely absent . . . because the change is an organic one, as regular and systemic as organic changes are, and not a passing phenomenon outside one's reckoning and power of minute observation.'

9.6 'The size and the shape of the brain remains the same, but there do occur subtle changes in biological composition of the cells and the nerve fibrils.'

9.7 'Subjectively, the flow of the essences, culled from the reproductive organs, can be distinctly felt in the space behind the palate, from the middle point to the root of the tongue. It pours into the cranium in an ambrosial stream so exquisitely pleasurable that even the rapture of love pales into insignificance when compared to it. At the same time, the erstwhile narrow-orbited consciousness is perceived spreading on all sides in ever-widening waves of lustrous being until it attains the dimensions of an effulgent unbounded ocean of awareness in which the wonderstruck ego, with only a faint recollection of its corporeal existence, appears like a dim and distant piece of floating corkwood, bobbing up and down, lost in the immensity of the expanse surrounding it.'

9.8 The secretions from the sexual organs 'are drawn up as if a powerful suction is applied from above to the nerves lining in the kanda (the triangular space below the navel and the muladhara chakra (plexus close to the anal opening). This marks the initiation of a new organic activity in which the brain, the nervous system, and the reproductive organs are the main participants in an effort to fashion the whole system to a new awareness beyond the normal limit of human consciousness.'

9.9 'The awakening of the kundalini takes two distinct forms. One is the upward flow of radiant energy that appears like a luminous glow in and around the head, and the other is the streaming of a fine biochemical essence into the brain and in the nerve centres of the vital organs. The latter manifestation gives rise to distinct sensations, both in the central canal, and the nerves affected by the movement.'

9.10 'I am convinced that the actual movements of the organic essence should be... measurable.' (Gopi Krishna, *Higher Consciousness*).

9.11 Gopi Krishna says 'There are negative as well as positive aspects of kundalini.' The positive aspects, of course, are the widening of consciousness and other features resulting in the transformation of a being. With regard to the negative aspects, he says, 'It also follows that since not all attempts at change in nature are successful, there must occur some cases in which the transformative processes do not lead to the desired end but result in psychosis and other mental disorders.'

9.12 According to Gopi Krishna, 'Knowledge of kundalini is not confined to India alone. It was known in almost all parts of the earth, including South America and Africa. The Caduceus of Mercury, which is an emblem of kundalini, was known in Assyria centuries before Egypt, under the name of the "Custodian of Tree of Life".... It is even held that the very word "kundalini" is derived from the Assyrian word "kundala" meaning coiled.'

9.13 The main thrust of Gopi Krishna in *Higher Consciousness* is that spiritual transformation is rooted in the body and is a product of sublimated sexual energy that shoots up, vitalises the brain and the nervous system and that this phenomenon must be and can be scientifically investigated. Gopi Krishna, however, affirms, 'The evolutionary mechanism, carrying us toward the unknown destination, with full awareness of the target to be achieved and full knowledge of all the infinitely complex biological changes necessary to attain this end, must be, as we can readily imagine, guided by a Superintelligence, beyond anything that we can conceive in human terms.'

The Transformation

9.14 Reference to Superintelligence is rare in Gopi Krishna's works. It is also noteworthy that Gopi Krishna says that guidance is provided by an agency that possesses superior intelligence. Unlike other spiritual philosophers, he does not seem to believe that guidance comes from the Divine.

9.15 Kundalini, also known, as the Serpent Power, according to N.B. Salunke (*The Times of India*, 2 April 2002) 'is in the form of a serpent with 3½ coils surrounding the Shiv Linga and is in the dormant posture. After its awakening, it traverses through the body (Spinal cord) – cleansing the six chakras and uniting with Shiv in the 7th chakra, Sahasrara. She is situated in the sacrum bone of the spinal cord. Sacrum – a Latin word, means sacred It is the last bone of the spinal cord.'

9.16 'Kundalini is trigunatmika. She is Mahalaxmi, Mahasaraswati and Mahakali.'

9.17 In their book *Why God Won't Go Away*, Andrew Newberg and Eugene d'Aquili present the view that if the brain was not constituted as it is, it would not be possible to have transcendental experiences. They say, 'The neurological machinery of transcendence may have arisen from the neural circuitry that evolved formatting and sexual experience.' In this respect, they advance the following arguments:

   a. The vocabulary used to describe sexual experience is the same as transcendental experience: 'bliss, rapture, ecstasy, and exaltation.'

b. The very neurological structures and pathways involved in transcendent experience – including the arousal, quiescent and limbic system – (were) evolved primarily to link sexual climax to the powerful sensation of orgasm.'

c. The mechanics involved in the two experiences are similar: 'repetitive, rhythmic stimulation. Significantly, orgasm requires the simultaneous stimulation of both the arousal and quiescent systems' as described in the note on 'Mysticism: General'.

Consciousness

1. **The Guru**

    The concept of guru originated in India and the reason for it must be the same as that of religion for the need of an intermediary.

    1.1 'There has been a lot of negative energy in the West on the word 'guru'. It has almost become pejorative. To be a "guru" is somehow to be a charlatan. To give your allegiance to a guru is to somehow give your power away.

    'Honoring your guru is not giving your power away. It is getting your power. For when you honour the guru . . . what you say is, "I see you." And what you see in another, you begin to see in yourself. It is outward evidence of your inner reality.' (Neale Donald Walsch, *Conversations with God*, Book 3).

    1.2 Walsch says that religion wants you to have an intermediary because religion does not want you to reach your Truth yourself. (Neale Donald Walsch, *Conversations with God*, Book 2).

1.3 'The first principle of true teaching is that nothing can be taught. The teacher is not an instructor or taskmaster, he is a helper and a guide. His business is to suggest and not to impose. . . . He does not impart knowledge . . . he shows (him) how to acquire knowledge for himself.' (Sri Aurobindo, 'The Hour of God', *Essays Divine and Human*).

1.4 The institution of gurus is firmly rooted in the Indian tradition. The etymological meaning of the word 'guru' is one who guides the shishya from darkness to light – the syllable 'gu' stands for darkness and 'ru' for light.

  a. In the olden times, a disciple stayed in an ashram, along with other disciples. Teaching was imparted suited to each disciple's temperament and capability.

  b. The guru was essentially a guide to show the path of self-realisation, different from upadhyaya, who was a formal teacher in worldly and practical arts. Others who performed ritual ceremonies were known as acharyas.

  c. According to Osho, 'The role of a guru is to give you glimpses of the real – not a teaching but an awakening. The guru is not a teacher but an awakener.' (Osho, 'From Maya (Illusion) to reality', *The Book of Secrets*).

  d. Sri Ramakrishna says, 'The Guru is a mediator. He brings man and God together; even as a matchmaker brings together the lover and the beloved. A Guru is like the mighty Ganges. Men throw all filth and refuse into the Ganges, but the holiness of that river is not diminished thereby. So is the Guru above all petty insult and censure.'

1.5   L.M. Dixit on guru:
   a.   L.M. Dixit, in an article in the *Times of India* dated 18 February 2002, defines a guru as a 'spiritual powerhouse'. 'Spiritualism is not scholarly exposition of religious doctrines or theories. It is not talk. It is the relationship between the soul and god and between the soul and other souls. . . . Only a realised soul knows the language of transmission. Only such a person can recognise a worthy soul for spiritual transmission.'
   b.   Normally the gurus prescribe a number of musts, prerequisites as qualifying qualities for acceptances of a seeker of spiritual development. According to Dixit, however, 'In Siddha Yoga inner growth occurs naturally and spontaneously. One of the unusual aspects of Siddha Yoga is that it not only gives rise to spiritual experiences but also creates the desire to lead a disciplined spiritual life.'
   c.   According to Dixit, a guru can transmit spiritual power in four ways: by touch, initiation, (transmission of spiritual energy), though looks and through thought. 'In all four cases it is essential that the receiver should be in a state of readiness.'
1.6   Guru as an obstruction in change:
   a.   There are two types of problems or obstacles in the development of transformational changes. One type are the general problems, common or generic and the other are particular ones, peculiar to an individual that bear the stamp of the individual's physical,

mental and emotional characteristics. The gurus, both individual and institutional and more so the institutional, deal with generic problems and developments. Their methods of instructions ignore the individual and since meditation is the science of inner self, their methods and teachings are at best superficial and at worst misleading and potentially harmful.

b. As far as individual gurus are concerned, see 'The Force Stage One'.

1.7 In the paper titled, 'Integral Psychology' contributed at the Second International Conference on Integral Psychology in Puducherry, Bahman A.K. Shirazi says that uniqueness of an individual 'may be best understood in terms of two ancient yogic principles of svabhava and svadharma. Svabhava refers to the fact that each individual is the resultant of a unique set of qualities and characteristics that are not replicable in their exact configuration. Svadharma implies that there is a unique path of development, growth and unfoldment for each individual which must be understood in terms of that person's svabhava.'

2. Experiences

2.1 Sri Aurobindo had been named by the as 'the most dangerous man in India' by Lord Minot, the Viceroy of British India. Sri Aurobindo says that on 15 February 1910, he 'received a command from above, in a voice well known to me, in three words: "Go to Chandernagore".' Just after that he was informed that that a warrant of arrest had been issued against him. (Sri Aurobindo, *On Himself*). He adds, 'I had accepted the rule of following the inner guidance implicitly and moving only as I was moved by the Divine.'

There is remarkable similarity between my own experiences and Sri Aurobindo's. Directives to me were also cryptic, just a few words.

2.2 'All my greatest experiences have come like that. I am in my usual consciousness and they come suddenly, as if to show their reality in the fullest contrast and vividness. They have the best value when first received this way.' (The Mother, *Mother India*).

My two experiences of 'dedicating my all' and 'to try me out' came suddenly, out of the blue.

2.3 Gopi Krishna in *Higher Consciousness*:

a. Gopi Krishna questions the genuineness of all visionary and auditory experiences. He believes that in 'a highly expanded state of consciousness (one) should be prone to visions of some sort where the pattern is already set by the ideas and notions habitual to him. But it is important to remember that all these visionary experiences with shape, form, place or time are but the figment of one's own imagination, rendered vivid and realistic by the radiant stream of (expanded consciousness).'

b. Gopi Krishna has a valid view. However, he does not talk of a sudden command or a sudden offering which are totally opposite to habitual ideas.

Bibliography

Basu, Arabinda, 'Sri Aurobindo's Metaphysical Psychology: A Brief Introduction', paper presented at the Second International Conference on Integral Psychology, held at Puducherry, 4–7 January 2001. The text has been published in Cornelissen, Matthijs, Ed., *Consciousness and Its Transformation* (SAICE, 2001).

Basu, Soumitra, 'Integral Psychotherapy: Personal Encounters', paper in the Second International Conference on Integral Psychology, held at Puducherry, 4–7 January 2001. The text has been published in Cornelissen, Matthijs, Ed., *Consciousness and Its Transformation* (SAICE, 2001).

Geller, Uri, 'The Physical Aspects of Higher Consciousness', *UriGeller.com*, https://www.urigeller.com/physical-aspects-higher-consciousness/.

Kent, J.T., *Homoeopathic Philosophy*.

Krishna, Gopi, *Higher Consciousness*.

Krishna, Gopi, *Kundalini: The Secret of Yoga*.

La Mere, *Glimpses of the Mother's Life*, Volume 2.

Leadbeater, C.W., *The Chakras*.

Bibliography

Matthew, V. George, 'Models of Consciousness and Its Transformation', paper presented at the Second International Conference on Integral Psychology, held at Puducherry, 4–7 January 2001. The text has been published in Cornelissen, Matthijs, Ed., *Consciousness and Its Transformation* (SAICE, 2001).

Miovic, Michael, 'Towards a Spiritual Psychology: Bridging Psychodynamic Psychotherapy with Integral Yoga', paper presented at the Second International Conference on Integral Psychology, held at Puducherry, 4–7 January 2001. The text has been published in Cornelissen, Matthijs, Ed., *Consciousness and Its Transformation* (SAICE, 2001).

Mohan, K. Krishna, 'Spirituality and Well Being: An Overview', paper presented at the Second International Conference on Integral Psychology, held at Puducherry, 4–7 January 2001. The text has been published in Cornelissen, Matthijs, Ed., *Consciousness and Its Transformation* (SAICE, 2001).

Newberg, Andrew and Eugene d'Aquili, *Why God Won't Go Away*.

Salunke, N.B., 'Raising Kundalini with Sahaj Yog', *The Times of India*, 2 April 2002, http://www.adishakti.org/pdf_files/rasing_kundalini_with_sahaj_yoga_(times_of_india).pdf.

Schnell, Donald, *The Initiation*.

Shirazi, Bahman A.K., 'Integral Psychology Metaphors and Processes of Personal Integration', paper presented at the Second International Conference on Integral Psychology, held at Puducherry, 4–7 January 2001. The text has been published in Cornelissen, Matthijs, Ed., *Consciousness and Its Transformation* (SAICE, 2001).

Sri Aurobindo, *Collected Poems*.

Sri Aurobindo, *Essays Divine and Human*.

Sri Aurobindo, *On Himself.*

Sri Aurobindo, 'The Hour of God', *Essays Divine and Human.*

Sri Aurobindo, *The Synthesis of Yoga.*

Thakkar, Vimala, *Personal Discovery of Truth.*

The Mother, *Mother India.*

The Mother, *Questions and Answers 1956* (*Collected Works of The Mother,* Volume 8).

Tolle, Eckhart, *The Power of Now.*

Van Vrekhem, Georges, *The Mother.*

Walsch, Neale Donald, *Conversations with God,* Book 2 and 3.